Something
That May
Shock
and
Discredit
You

Also by Daniel Mallory Ortberg

The Merry Spinster: Tales of Everyday Horror
Texts from Jane Eyre

Something That May Shock and Discredit You

and

Discredit You

ATRIA BOOKS

New York   London   Toronto   Sydney   New Delhi

ATRIA
BOOKS

An Imprint of Simon & Schuster, Inc.
1230 Avenue of the Americas
New York, NY 10020

First Atria Books hardcover edition February 2020

ATRIA BOOKS and colophon are trademarks of Simon & Schuster, Inc.

For information about special discounts for bulk purchases,
please contact Simon & Schuster Special Sales at 1-866-506-1949
or business@simonandschuster.com.

The Simon & Schuster Speakers Bureau can bring authors to
your live event. For more information or to book an event, contact
the Simon & Schuster Speakers Bureau at 1-866-248-3049
or visit our website at www.simonspeakers.com.

Interior design by Michelle Marchese

Manufactured in the United States of America

1   3   5   7   9   10   8   6   4   2

Library of Congress Cataloging-in-Publication Data is available.

ISBN 978-1-9821-0521-1
ISBN 978-1-9821-0523-5 (ebook)

To Grace Elisabeth Lavery,
who refuses to carry an umbrella

Contents

CHAPTER 1

When You Were Younger and You Got Home Early and You Were the First One Home and No One Else Was Out on the Street, Did You Ever Worry That the Rapture Had Happened without You? I Did.

O ne generally grows up thinking about the Rapture a great deal or not at all. Most don't, I think, but among those who did, there's always the question of how, if at all, to bring up the subject in mixed company, whether in the hopes of eliciting either laughter or shock, followed by sexual intrigue mingled with pity. It's easy enough to sell out an evangelical Christian childhood, and plenty of other pens have been given over to the subject of whether it's a good idea to raise children in the expectation of being swept up by the Raisin Bran scoop of heaven; I have no wish to dwell on the question of whether I ought to have been taught about the Rapture. No one consulted me beforehand, and I can't see why I should be asked to provide an opinion on the subject now. I was roughly as afraid of the Rapture as I was of being the last person in the house who left the basement at nighttime and had to turn the lights out before I went up the stairs—it felt variously real and ridiculous depending on how close I was to being alone. Afternoons when I was the first person to come home after school and the neighborhood seemed slightly emptier than usual were ideal for Rapture practice, for seeing if I could gin up sufficient panic and remorse at the prospect of being *un*scooped; playing DC Talk's cover of "I Wish We'd All Been Ready" sometimes helped, but more often than not just made me even more self-conscious of having to trick myself into getting in the mood.

I was aware, too, that my parents' theology did not have much room for the kind of guessing-games- and crossword-puzzle-style approach to eschatology popular among many white evangelicals in the 1990s, that if I were to press them for details about the End Times trivia I had absorbed by virtue of growing up in the suburban Midwest they would at best dismiss it and at worst ask where on earth I'd picked up such things. I had a sharp sense for when keeping a secret would result in a pleasanter outcome, and preferred to occasionally play out Rapture-like scenarios in private than have them either confirmed or debunked by outside opinion. I could have a Rapture a day if I liked—as long as I never asked my parents' permission to go Rapturing—and dedicated a number of afternoons to making myself dizzy imagining the day when time would burst and unspool itself in every possible direction, and all those willing to be perfected would be milled down by the grindstone of heaven in a lovely, terrifying roar.

At least part of the reason I never asked anyone questions about the fears and desires that preoccupied me was a peculiar certainty that to invite details would destroy anything I hoped for; that the loveliness of being pressed directly against God's heart and melted down into holiness would become ridiculous if a start date were ever announced. And I did fear it, often, for as much as I longed to be seized, swept up, and changed without or even against my will, I also dreaded it. I was possessed of a rootless homesickness that translated quite neatly, for a religious eleven-year-old, into heaven-longing; later it would translate quite neatly, for a nervous thirty-one-year-old, into transsexuality.

"Of that day"—*Rapture Day, hey-YouTube-this-is-my-voice-six-days-on-T day*, according to the book of Matthew, chapter 24—"and the hour no one knows, not even the angels of heaven, but My Father only." Just as the days of Noah were, so also will the coming of the Son of Man be. For as in the days before the flood, they were eating and drinking, marrying and giving in marriage, until the day that Noah entered the ark, and did not know until the flood came and took them all away, so also will the coming of the Son of Man be.

In the early days of my transition (when "transition" consisted mostly of refusing to wash my clothes, letting them pile up on the floor so I could weep in bed, getting significant haircuts, and responding incredibly tersely if any of my friends acknowledged that I'd cut my hair in any way), I often described my sudden shift in self-awareness as feeling as if a demon had entered my room in the middle of the night, startled me awake by whispering, "What if you were a man, sort of?" into my ear, then slithered out the window before I could ask any follow-up questions. I had been eating and drinking, working and laying work aside, and then the floodwaters prevailed exceedingly on the earth, and all the high hills under the whole heaven were covered. All flesh died that moved upon the earth, birds and cattle and beasts and every creeping thing that creeps on the earth, and every man, all in whose nostrils was the breath of the spirit of life, all that was on the dry land, died and were destroyed from the earth. And the waters prevailed on the earth one hundred and fifty days. Sometimes cis people will describe a sense of loss at the transition of a loved one and describe it as mourning a kind of death, but I think they've got it the wrong way round. It was if everything on the earth was dead and dying except for me, and that none of the practice runs I'd ever rehearsed in childhood had prepared me for it.

I revisited my own childhood constantly for anything that would be sufficient to make sense of my present situation and was frustrated once again by my own calculated, dreamy vagueness; how like me not to keep a written record of anything I might later like to read. No one knows the hour of the coming of the Son of Man (who might start asking questions), so it's best to travel light. It was such a ridiculous and yet a persistent thought, which came on all at once and in a way that suggested it had always been with me: *What if you were a man, sort of?* To which the only response imaginable was *What if I were anything? What if I were Donkey Kong, or the city of Chicago?* Nothing in my life previous could have prepared me for this question, and I was unqualified to answer it. It was a ridiculous thought to think, and a ridiculous feeling to feel, and yet there it was, so often lurking just beneath something else: What if you were a man, sort of?

Riddle-posing night-demons, the happy days of Noah, the hour of the Son of Man—one of the many advantages of a religious childhood is the variety of metaphors made available to describe untranslatable inner experiences. A few years later, with a transition slightly less bed-centered, I might have described that feeling instead as this: after a number of years being vaguely troubled by an inconsistent, inexplicable sense of homesickness, I woke up one morning and remembered my home address, having forgotten even that I forgot it in the first place, then grown fearful and weary at even the prospect of trying to get back. I have often had a relationship to men that has been bewildering to me. I have been sometimes too charged with an emotion I cannot name, and tried to get them to relate to me in a way that was not easily recognizable, either to them or to me. Had I been in any way prepared for that moment of question-asking, I would have arranged my life in such a way that the moment would have never come. I never saw it coming, so I was never ready; then it was over.

The timeline of awaiting a rapture is broken into two parts: First one becomes willing to be stolen away, then one waits patiently for it to happen, occasionally topping up one's own willingness and preparedness if stores seem to be running low. But the forces of heaven do the lifting, the heavy work, the spiriting away, the catching up of the body in the air. The timeline of transition is both alike and nothing like it: one becomes, if not willing to transition, at least curious, sometimes desperate, sometimes terrified, sometimes confident, sometimes tentative. Then, at some point, one has to do or say something in order to make it happen. The force of my desire to transition, when I allowed myself to be hit with the full force of it, felt so supernatural and overwhelming it was as if all I had to do was stand and wait and somehow the process would begin itself around me, first the lifting, then the heavy work, then the catching up of the body in the air, then the translation from the corruptible to the incorruptible. My own desires had seemed external to me—I certainly couldn't remember *deciding* to want anything—so it stood to reason that whatever came next would happen *to* me rather than *because* of me.

"Then two will be in the field: one will be taken and the other left. Two women will be grinding flour at the mill: one will be taken and the other left. Watch therefore, for you do not know what hour your Lord is coming. But know this, that if the master of the house had not known what hour the thief would come, he would have watched and not suffered his house to be broken into. Therefore you also be ready, for you know not what hour your Lord comes." I had not foreseen the hour when I would be struck by transition-longing. How then could I be asked to discern what came next? I hoped with all my heart to wait long enough for my desires to pass, or to be remade at someone else's hands. "For God was pleased through Him to reconcile to Himself all things, whether things on earth or things in heaven, by making peace" (Col. 1:20). Everyone will be reconciled through peace and pleasure who can possibly stand it. If you don't squeeze through the door at first, just wait patiently for Heaven to grind you into a shape that fits.

Chapter Titles from the On the Nose, Po-Faced Transmasculine Memoir I Am Trying Not to Write

The first step in writing a book is not writing the wrong book. The fight against writing *Son of a Preacher Man: Becoming Daniel Mallory Ortberg, My Journey Trekking Through the Transformative Expedition of Emergence, Voyaging Shiftward Into Form—An Odyssey in Two Sexes: Pilgrimage to Ladhood* must be renewed every day. I am tempted always to make some force or organization outside of myself responsible for my own discomfort, to retroactively apply consistency to my sense of self as a child, to wax poetic about something in order to cover up uncertainty, to overshare in great detail out of fear that the details will be dragged out of me if I don't volunteer them first, and to lapse into cliché in order to get what I want as quickly as possible.

Chapter One: An Outdoor Picnic Signifying the Successful Reintegration into the Family Unit, and a Flashback
A description of the author, naked, at five, then again at twelve, then again at twenty, then again at thirty-two.

Chapter Two: A Mostly Forced Poetic Description of My
                Hormone Delivery System
*This is my voice four seconds on T. This is my voice after saying, "This
is my voice four seconds on T," so probably another seven seconds on T.
This is the molecular structure of testosterone. This is a rhapsodic list of
side effects.*

Chapter Three: My Male Privilege? My Male Privilege Seems
                So Tenuous
But I'm also scared about my male privilege!

Chapter Four: *Extreme Paula Cole Voice* Where Have All the
                Tomboys Gone?
*I'm sorry I lured the tomboys away to Boy Island. I am heartily sorry for
my fault, my fault, my grievous fault, and I promise to make a good-faith
error at restitution, returning at least five tomboys or their cash equivalent.*

Chapter Five: An Extensive Water-Based Metaphor
*Trans people: Always mesmerized, held, fascinated, and ultimately
defeated by reflective surfaces. What's that, you say? A mirror of some
kind? Hold it up to me so I might gaze at it with longing and dissatisfaction.*

Chapter Six: Have You Heard of . . . ? Mermaids/Centaurs/Sirens/
                Sphinxes/Butterflies/Snakes/Werewolves/Any
                Other Cryptid? Well, You're Going to Hear About
                Them Now.
They're like me!!

Chapter Seven: Maiden, Mother, Crone, Mothman, Hans
                Moleman
*Room to work in a Golden Bough reference, maybe? Joseph Campbell,
at the very least.*

Chapter Eight: Footnotes, for Legitimacy
In which the author clearly feels obligated to badly summarize theory in order to offer a publicly defensible sense of self.

Chapter Nine: An Exhaustive Recounting of Every Crush I Have Ever Had, Tagged and Exhibited, Followed by Six Pages of Layman's Chemistry
In which the author has grown a thin, dreadful mustache, which the reader can intuitively sense through the page.

Chapter Ten: What If Masculinity, but in a Soft, Sort-of-Drapey Jacket
That'd be nice, right? Maybe in velvet; I don't know. It's soft now! We can all enjoy it this way.

Chapter Eleven: In Which I Interview Every Man Who Refused to Walk Through a Door I Held Open for Them Before Transition and Inform Them that They Are Retroactively Gay Now
If I'm honest—which I'm not—I did it for male attention. (Both the opening of doors and transition.)

Chapter Twelve: "Liminal"
In which the author refers to himself, alternately, as a "gender rebel," "smuggler," "real-life-sexual-crossing-guard," and, for some reason, a cyborg.

Chapter Thirteen: In Which I Rescue Masculinity by Taking Up Weight Lifting, Heroically
It's subversive and important when I do it.

CHAPTER 2

My Brothers, My Brothers, My Brothers' Keepers, My Brothers, My Brothers, My Brothers and Me

And Isaac loved Esau because he ate of his game, but Rebecca loved Jacob.

Now Jacob cooked a stew, and Esau came in weary from the field. And Esau said to Jacob, "Please feed me with that same red stew, for I am weary" (therefore his name was called Edom).

But Jacob said, "First sell me your birthright."

Esau said, "I am about to die; of what use is a birthright to me?"

Jacob said, "Swear to me first."

So he swore to him, and sold his birthright to Jacob. And Jacob gave Esau bread and stew of lentils; then he ate and drank, arose and went his way. Thus Esau despised his birthright.

—Gen. 25:28–34

Before I began to transition, I tried my very best not to transition, for the following reasons.

It might be well and good for other people, but I was uniquely unqualified.

I could not trust either my knowledge of myself or my own desires.

I could not trust my own happiness, such that if transition were to produce a new kind of peace or serenity within me, it would merely be further evidence of my capacity for self-deception, just another setup before an increasingly long fall.

I was too old, had in fact been too old since the age of twelve.

I was used to being a woman, and I *liked* women and couldn't imagine my transition as anything other than an act of—at the very least—impoliteness toward women.

I would lose my family.

Cis men would be indifferent and cruel to me if I did.

I would lose my sense of self and my place in the world.

Transition wouldn't work on me anyway.

I had worked out a sort of tortured mathematical equation in favor of never making a decision or sharing my feelings with anyone—I was just susceptible enough to the rhetoric of transition to make my continued existence as a cis woman unbearable, but *insufficiently trans* to guarantee that actual transition would bring with it any relief, which meant that my only option was to suffer in silence. The more I longed to transition, the stronger the evidence that I should not do it; the very fact that I desired it to the exclusion of all other desires meant that I was being stubborn and irrational and in need of restraint. I knew I could not trust my own feelings, because I had not always been aware of a desire to transition, so I could not allow myself to make a decision now on the basis of any feeling, however strong. I also had the sense that there was something distinctly impolite about it, like agreeing to go out for pizza with a group of friends and, just as we were being led to our table, announcing, "I think I'd rather have birthday cake for dinner. Does anyone mind if we leave now and go bake a cake somewhere?" And my friends *might* agree out of politeness and affection, but their hearts wouldn't really be in it, and I would in fact have trespassed on their good natures by asking, making such an outrageous, selfish request.

To which the obvious response, of course, is that the body is not a pizza, except for when it is, and I was not wrong to fear that other people would take my body personally, as indeed some people always have. For so many years I was easily able to dismiss the question of whether I had any particular opinions or preferences when it came to my own body under the comfortable rubric that *most* women disliked their bodies, because of sexism and through no fault of their own, and that the best thing one could do in that situation, if self-acceptance seemed overly ambitious, was to keep it to oneself since everyone else was suffering in the same way. At the age of eleven or twelve I had become dimly aware that something had stalled with my pubescence: I had been taken to a doctor; diagnosed with a common, treatable hormonal disorder called polycystic ovarian syndrome; and placed on a regimen of feminizing hormones I would take without questioning for the next eighteen years. I had grown comfortable at the thought of my body as a public resource that I was responsible for holding in trust. I had been charged with its maintenance and general upkeep, and on the strength of such a relationship had been able to develop a certain vague fondness for it, while also maintaining a pleasant distance. *Don't ask me; I just work here,* was my attitude. *I can let the supervisors know when there's a problem and they tell me how to fix it.*

I don't mean to suggest that either the doctors or my parents behaved thoughtlessly at the time. Had I voiced any objection to the treatment, I have every reason to believe I would have been listened to, but it had not yet occurred to me that I might object at all. In fact, had someone asked me every day and every night of my life, "What are you?" I would have said, "I'm a girl," every time. There were many ways to be a good woman, I knew, and having grown up in the 1990s meant I'd heard sufficient variations on the sentiment that women could do anything—I had not been so covetous of boys' toys or men's jeans that I grew confused and assumed that meant there was nothing for it but to start a regime of masculinizing hormones and change my name. Women could do anything they liked. We all of us lived in a world where transition was unthought of, so we did not think of it—I could no sooner blame them than myself. I disliked sexism, admired and liked women, had been given a girl's name, and found it very easy not to think about my body; surely this made me a girl, and certainly no one had ever suggested this was anything less than sufficient. Other people occasionally liked my body (plenty objected to it, but again this seemed like proof for, rather than against, my womanhood), I liked it when others were pleased; to me this was the same as liking the thing itself.

But the reasoning did not hold, the distance was unsupportable, the ruse susceptible; there came a point in my life when I could no longer pretend that I wanted nothing. As soon as I allowed myself to consider the possibility of transition, not as it related to other people but as it related to me, I had to fight not to transition every day. Then there was a long and tiresome fight against myself; eventually the fight ended. (For more details on the fight, turn to chapter 6.)

The first practical question to be settled once the matter of transition became inevitable was exactly how much testosterone to take, and for how long. There is sometimes a tendency, at least among the trans men I have known, to treat testosterone therapy at the outset as if one were the first to order french fries at the table: tentative, looking to others for guidance and support, a half-frantic desire not to be the only one. *If I have some, will you have some? I know* you'll *have some—is it possible to get a half order? This is for the table, not just for me. What's the smallest actual amount of testosterone that you can medically offer me? I'll take that, but can you put half of it in a to-go box before you bring it out? I'm sharing with friends.* There is a number of excellent reasons why a person might want to do so, but for me it was only a hope to whittle down my transition to the absolute bare minimum. Whatever trans was, I was ready to accept it as a part of myself, but I was not unwilling to pay more than the cover charge. *Do you have trans on the menu? Is it possible to get a cup instead of a bowl? What's the smallest amount of trans you have available? I'll take that.* I wanted to transition; I had become convinced that it was essential to my happiness and well-being, but at the same time I remained sure that it was simultaneously going to ruin my life. My most desperate desire was not that I would be assisted in my transition but that someone would either force or forbid me to do it, because I could not take responsibility for annihilating my own life. Having finally admitted to wanting something was bad enough; the least I felt I could do was want very little of it. None of which is to say that there is, or ought to be, a transition continuum running from "lots/most/maximal" to "least/less/minimal," merely that I have only ever admitted what I hunger for under duress, when all of my other options have been exhausted and my escape routes cut off, and even then seek to downplay the nature of it in advance, the better to ward off disappointment. (And after all that, it turned out it *was* possible to get a half order of testosterone for the transitioner with the moderate appetite.)

So there was a great flurry of agitation and argument in the days before I took testosterone. I feared that it would not work at all; I feared that it would work too well; I feared that what I thought of as "working" actually meant "feeling good all of the time," an impossible request of any hormone, sexed or otherwise. I made bargains with my will and my endocrine system; I hedged; I placed bets; I predicted; I agonized; I demanded reassurance and implausible promises from everyone I knew who had ever picked up a prescription. I could not imagine a worse condition for myself, so it cheered me somewhat to imagine that starting testosterone would confirm that I did not in fact need it so that I could all the sooner shake myself from this delusion and find something else to worry about.

What happened instead was the discovery of what I might call *vocational clarity*—not an unassailable certainty founded on decades of unwavering identification, nor yet a preternatural calm, but an ever-deepening, ever-widening sense of peace and purpose and delight. I might have mistrusted certainty after such a prolonged period of turbulence. The will of God when the time comes to apportion tasks is not always fixed, at least not in the tradition of the people of God. So Mary asks, "How can this be?" of her messenger, so Gideon lays out a fleece on the threshing floor, so Sarah laughs at the impossibility of her body, so Saul hides himself among the supplies. In everything give thanks, do not quench the spirit, do not despise prophecies, test all things, and hold fast to what is good (1 Thess. 5:18–21). Transition had not always been true of me, but I found that the more place I allowed it in my life, the further back it cast its roots. Whether or not the birthright had been mine to begin with or ever intended for me, I found the burden easy and the yoke light.

After the settling into vocation always comes the awkwardness of growth. I took a new name based primarily on how well it sounded when called out in a coffee shop; where I'd once had a fairly unique woman's name (shared only with the older sister from *Family Ties*), I now found myself with a relatively commonplace one for a man—moreover, that there was already a writer named

Daniel Mallory, who had recently made headlines for signing a million-dollar book advance and, apparently, fabricating stories about his personal life in order to inflate his professional reputation. Having my cis doppelgänger called publicly to account for charmingly committing lightweight fraud while I was in the early stages of transition sums up a whole host of transmasculine anxiety! Then, too, there was the testosterone-born neck acne to be dealt with, which demanded its own attendant rituals and acts of soothing. Always there was the suspicion of my own peacefulness—yes, this brings me joy and energy and clarity today, and yesterday, too, but tomorrow is certainly the day the legs are swept out from under me, and I'll have to run home begging for forgiveness. It is difficult for the mind to unlearn certain anxieties.

The other day I was talking with a friend about the gradual but profound change testosterone has had on my voice, and I found myself saying something I say a lot nowadays: "You know, I used to have a lovely singing voice." Which is mostly true, but "lovely" is fairly subjective, and it was only lovely by singing-in-the-shower or gathered-round-the-family-piano standards, not church-solo or sudden-appearance-at-an-open-mic standards. I sometimes worry I sound like I am making claims to having been a great beauty or the king of the Franks, the passing of time being sufficient for everyone to accept the polite fiction. And how will I know when I've dipped into fabulism if I don't keep in constant contact with my past selves? Who is going to oppose me: "No, you always had limited breath control and sounded obviously strained the moment you strayed out of your comfortable half-octave range, you acne-ridden deceiver"?

Some of it, I think, is self-conscious cover; starting testosterone did not mean I immediately left the house looking like a full-grown man in his thirties, I mostly just looked like myself, only hairier and slightly puffier in the cheeks. Generally, there was a mild social cost to be paid for going out in public looking that way. And some of it also comes from an urge to prove that I didn't transition out of necessity but desire: *Being a woman is hard, but I was good at it,* I think is the underlying anxiety. *Nobody fired me; I quit. I know I'm not trying to look pretty anymore, and I apologize to all those who have to look at me, because I used to try and I'm not enough of a man yet for it not to be a problem. I promise to work very hard to look like Victor Garber so you can look at a handsome man in three years' time minimum.* If my appearance was a common resource held in public trust, the least I could do was hang up a sign: *Please pardon our dust during refurbishment. We're working hard to update the site you've so often enjoyed.*

But there's also a slightly perverse pleasure to be taken in speaking so proudly about the past, and it's a pleasure I've seen other trans people take for themselves, mentioning—possibly even exaggerating slightly, as our past selves are unlikely to walk through the door in contradiction—how good we used to look or whatever it was that people thought we were. It may be in part because we are so often accused of simply misunderstanding gender stereotypes that we can take pleasure in reminiscing about how well we have sometimes fit in. *Kids, Daddy used to have the greatest rack in the tristate area.* I find this habit very endearing; transitioning often makes room for fondness where there was no room before. Pride without ownership, affection without desire, that's what I'm trying to communicate when I say something like "I used to have a great ass." Maybe, too, an attempt to say I'm a rational actor. I can see things as they are; I can assign proportionate value to things; I'm making these decisions with a sound mind and an accurate view of reality. It may be nothing more than an attempt to forestall that kindest and most painful of denials, *But you used to be such a _____. But you had such a beautiful _____.* I know, don't remind me. She was lovely, and she had such nice hair.

One of the things women do well as a group—I speak broadly here but not definitively, many women don't, and plenty of women do it well sometimes and in some situations and not at all well in others—is layer relationships one on top of the other, doubling back and reinforcing and looping multiple ties into one. In this way transitioning can sometimes feel like pulling apart an entire web, inconveniencing (at the very least) a number of other women who had relied on your position in order to maintain theirs. This may be a very self-centered way to regard one's transition; I'm sure many people who transition don't feel this way at all. Nor do I mean to suggest I've toppled any woman out of her own life by taking testosterone or changing my name. But I've spent more of my time than I ought to preparing for an exit interview with womanhood that will never happen. No one is calling me to account or asking why, after thirty years in the position, I was moving into a different role in the company.

But most of my growing-up was spent being trained for a job I no longer have, and I never quite knew how to express my love and gratitude for the ways I was treated as a woman, by women, while no longer continuing to be one. I had a lovely singing voice once, nothing special but quite pleasant to listen to. My range has narrowed now, and my voice cracks on most notes above middle C, but I have reason to believe it will settle into something mellow someday, both different and continuous. Nobody is asking me to apologize for anything, but I still want to, if only for the pleasure and the sweetness and the release of being forgiven.

I tried apologizing to my mother when I told her I was not just "figuring some things out" but transitioning. It was one thing to be a man, or *wish* to be a man, or *live* as a man, in a coffee shop or with a friend or alone in my apartment or out in public, but to be a man in relation with my mother meant being not-her-daughter.

A person is not-a-daughter in their own right; they are a daughter *to* and *of* someone else, and as much as I knew my gender was my own, that my vocation was assured, that self-determination mattered more to me than external validation—still if I could have transitioned while remaining her daughter, I would have wanted to do so. I wanted to promise I would not change in relation to her, that I remained grateful for the girlhood she had given me, that her affection for my former embodiment, my former name, would not hurt me, that if I could have stayed a woman a minute longer I would have done it.

I wanted to promise that this would be the last change, that I would never make excessive demands on the people who I believed were bound to love me, believing as I did that their loving and my changing was somehow a rupture or a violation of the agreement I had entered into by being born. I thought often of Jacob and Esau. Of all the brothers in Genesis who deny and disinherit one another, they are the first to reconcile. Cain flees from the body of Abel, Isaac and Ishmael are parted as children and never meet again, but Jacob and Esau make peace. Before they make peace, Jacob changes his name.

Jacob arose that night and took his two wives, his two female servants, and his eleven sons, and crossed over the ford of Jabbok. He took them, sent them over the brook, and sent over what he had. Then Jacob was left alone; and a man wrestled with him until the breaking of day. Now when the man saw that he did not prevail against him, he touched the socket of his hip; and the socket of Jacob's hip was out of joint as he wrestled with him. And he said, "Let me go, for the day breaks."

But Jacob said, "I will not let you go unless you bless me!"

So the man said to him, "What is your name?"

He said, "Jacob."

And the man said, "Your name shall no longer be called Jacob, but Israel; for you have struggled with God and with men, and have prevailed."

Then Jacob asked, saying, "Tell me your name, I pray."

And he said, "Why is it that you ask about my name?" And he blessed him there.

So Jacob called the name of the place Peniel: "For I have seen God face to face, and my life is preserved." Just as he crossed over Peniel the sun rose on him, and he limped on his hip.

This part of Jacob's story begins abruptly. The angel does not appear or announce himself—in one moment he is *not there*, and in the next moment he is *there and wrestling with Jacob*. He refuses to name or explain himself; the two are alone as they struggle, on the far side of the river from the rest of Jacob's family. Jacob is not overcome, but his body is marked by the encounter, and he moves differently throughout the world forever after. Jacob is given a blessing and a new name but never an explanation; the angel is gone as abruptly as it came; Jacob never walks the same. Trying not to transition was the hardest work in the world. The nicest thing about transition was letting go.

After Jacob crosses the river, he is reunited with his brother, Esau, for the first time in years—Esau, whose birthright he maneuvered out of him; Esau, whose forgiveness is not assured. Jacob bows to the ground seven times, uncertain of his welcome, but Esau runs to meet him "and embraced him, and fell on his neck and kissed him, and they wept." Jacob offers Esau gifts, and Esau refuses on the grounds that he already has more than enough. I was as desperate to remain legible to my family of origin according to their terms as I was desperate to change, as desperate for permission as I was for autonomy. I could not rid myself of the idea that my body was in some fixed and ultimate way the property of my parents, a collective asset of the family unit. More unthinkable than the idea of transitioning was the idea of transitioning outside of my family—of failing to become a son, if I asked sweetly and often enough and worked very hard to earn it. As a child I sometimes attempted to bargain for bigger and better birthday presents by promising "It will be my birthday and Christmas present combined—I'll never ask for anything else again—this is the only thing I'll ever want, I swear." There is a limit to gift-giving, and there is a limit to gift-getting, and I sensed myself getting dangerously close to that boundary. So Jacob offers his gifts to Esau again: "'Please, if I have now found favor in your sight, then receive my present from my hand, inasmuch as I have seen your face as though I had seen the face of God, and you were pleased with me. Please take my blessing that is brought to you, because God has dealt graciously with me, and because I have enough.' So he urged him, and he took it." Jacob and Esau do not meet again after this; less a gift exchange than a formal buyout of shares in the family business.

Help Me, Brother, or I Sink

John Bunyan's *The Pilgrim's Progress* is one of the bestselling books of all time; there was a moment where Protestant households could be reliably counted on to have a copy of the *Progress* and a copy of the Bible, if nothing else. I received a copy of my very own for my eighth birthday. Near the end of the first part the man Christian and his companion Hopeful find themselves at the very gate of their destination, the Celestial City. After passing through every possible trial, they come to an unfordable river.

> Now I further saw that betwixt them and the gate was a river; but there was no bridge to go over: the river was very deep. At the sight, therefore, of this river, the pilgrims were much astounded; but the men that went with them said, "You must go through, or you cannot come at the gate."
>
> The pilgrims then, especially Christian, began to despond in their minds and looked this way and that, but no way could be found by them by which they might escape the river. Then they asked the men if the waters were all of a depth. They said, "No"; yet they could not help them in that case, for said they, "You shall find it deeper or shallower as you believe in the King of the place."

They then addressed themselves to the water; and entering, Christian began to sink. And crying out to his good friend Hopeful, he said, "I sink in deep waters, the billows go over my head; all his waves go over me."

Then said the other, "Be of good cheer, my brother; I feel the bottom, and it is good."

Then said Christian, "Ah! my friend, the sorrows of death have compassed me about; I shall not see the land that flows with milk and honey."

And with that a great darkness and horror fell upon Christian, so that he could not see before him; also here he, in great measure, lost his senses, so that he could neither remember nor orderly talk of any of those sweet refreshments that he had met with in the way of his pilgrimage. But all the words that he spake still tended to discover that he had horror of mind, and hearty fears that he should die in that river, and never obtain entrance in at the gate; here also, as they that stood by perceived, he was much in the troublesome thoughts of the sins that he had committed, both since and before he began to be a pilgrim.

'Twas also observed that he was troubled with apparitions of hobgoblins and evil spirits; for ever and anon he would intimate so much by words. Hopeful, therefore, here had much ado to keep his brother's head above water; yea, sometimes he would be quite gone down, and then ere awhile he would rise up again half dead. Hopeful also would endeavour to comfort him, saying, "Brother, I see the gate, and men standing by it to receive us."

But Christian would answer, "'Tis you, 'tis you they wait for; you have been hopeful ever since I knew you."

"And so have you," said he to Christian.

"Ah, brother," said he, "surely, if I was right, he would now arise to help me; but, for my sins, he hath brought me into the snare, and hath left me."

Then said Hopeful, "These troubles and distresses that you go through in these waters are no sign that God hath forsaken you; but are sent to try you, whether you will call to mind that which heretofore you have received of his goodness, and live upon him in your distresses."

Then I saw in my dream that Christian was as in a muse awhile, to whom also Hopeful added this word, "Be of good cheer, God maketh thee whole"; and with that Christian brake out with a loud voice,

"Oh, I see him again! and he tells me, 'When thou passest through the waters, I will be with thee; and through the rivers, they shall not overflow thee: when thou walkest through the fire, thou shalt not be burned; neither shall the flame kindle upon thee.'"

Then they both took courage, and the enemy was after that as still as a stone, until they were gone over. Christian therefore presently found ground to stand upon; and so it followed that the rest of the river was but shallow. Thus they got over.

YOU AND ME AND OUR FIRST YEARS ON T

You: in possession of a leonine grace and sun-warmed sexual fluidity reminiscent of every kind and unattainable straight-boy crush I had in high school, have developed a robust individual response to overfishing that still prioritizes communal action, definitely has cum gutters, *could* post a lot of pictures of yourself at the gym but don't (but aren't self-consciously opposed to the practice), presently living in total harmony with any number of online subcultures I both resent and long to participate in, only developed a (non-embarrassing) beard after achieving total facial masculinization, has two boyfriends (one cis, one trans, both six

foot three), effortlessly made the switch from bravely disregarding female beauty standards to bravely disregarding male beauty
standards at the two-month mark, ported your account from HER
to Scruff the day before starting T, knows your size when ordering
shirts from ASOS, has a consistent shirt size, owns and uses the
correct number of skin-care products with tea tree oil in them,
gendered correctly and casually by everyone but would react with
disarming strength and grace if you ever happened to be misgen-
dered over the phone—it won't happen, but you *would* if it did—
somehow developed *more* hair at the crown of your head, uterus
acting normal, qualified for peri-areolar but somehow wound
up not needing top surgery after all—"I don't know what to say,
I used to be a 34D or something but they just . . . disappeared
after a while, go figure"—socially transitioned twelve years ago
but still younger than me, passes 100 percent of the time but still
gets the butch head nod on the street somehow, never uses judg-
mental language like "passing" even as a convenient shorthand,
remembered to freeze his eggs, non-embarrassing relationship
to transmasculine-resonant media properties like *Mulan* and *A
Separate Peace* and *The Lord of the Rings* live-action movies, looks
good in sweaters, comfortably five foot eight, friend to every living gender, never tiresome about astrology, has never written a
single personal essay, perfect M-shaped hairline, total feminist
trailblazer pre-transition and produces just the right amount of
laid-back and supportive male energy post-, living life to the full-
est, quietly jettisoned any personal habits that people would have
found intriguing in a girl but super irritating in a guy, "best thing
I ever did," never does unsolicited favors for others in order to
feel overlooked and aggrieved when they don't reciprocate even
though they never asked you to do them a favor in the first place,
loveth at all times and born for a time of adversity; when some

evildoers come to your household you call for a basin and begin
to wash their feet such that they are filled with confusion and
begin to do penance; some call you John the Baptist, others say
Elijah, and still others one of the prophets, but I say you are the
Son of Man—this was not revealed to me by flesh and blood but
by my Father in heaven, actually looks your age.

Me, on T for the exact same amount of time: regularly ma'amed
by birds, simultaneously an embarrassment to feminism and transmasculinity, personally responsible for the failures of the body-
positivity movement, forgot to have cheekbones, currently stuck
inside an airport bathroom, forgot to develop upper-body strength
or look into my reproductive options before filling my uterus with
old needles, fell in a pothole, problematic hamstrings, constantly
writing directionless personal essays about early transition mile-
stones that I'll regret in eight minutes, getting colds more frequently,
both twelve and forty at the same time, reinforcing the binary but
not in a cool subversive way, neck looking worse by the minute, forgot own pronouns; I baptize with water but there comes one after
me whose sandals I am not fit to untie.

**Me, sitting in the middle of a river and insisting on drowning
despite my companion's numerous protestations that (1) I can
touch the bottom, (2) help awaits us on the other side, and (3)
they have just made it through that part of the river and will happily help me to safety:** Other people are *legitimately trans* in a
mysterious and inchoate way that I am not (but don't ask me
what *legitimately trans* means because that would require developing a coherent worldview); I, on the other hand, merely cannot stop *thinking* about transitioning, which is not the same
thing, merely thinking about transitioning is distinct from
wanting to transition, as long as I'm the one doing the thinking;

which means that I am not trans, which means that I ought not to transition, which leaves me no option besides continuing to think endlessly about transition; if only I were trans, then I could transition—

You, handsomely: Be of good cheer; God maketh thee whole.

Repeat as necessary.

Thus, eventually, we get over.

CHAPTER 3

Apollo and Hyacinthus Die Playing Ultimate Frisbee, and I Died Watching Teenage Boys Play Video Games

His [Apollo's] zither and his bow no longer fill his eager mind and now without a thought of dignity, he carried nets and held the dogs in leash, and did not hesitate to go with Hyacinthus on the rough, steep mountain ridges; and by all of such associations, his love was increased.

Now Titan was about midway, betwixt the coming and the banished night, and stood at equal distance from those two extremes. Then, when the youth and Phoebus were well stripped, and gleaming with rich olive oil, they tried a friendly contest with the discus. First Phoebus, well-poised, sent it awhirl through air, and cleft the clouds beyond with its broad weight; from which at length it fell down to the earth, a certain evidence of strength and skill. Heedless of danger Hyacinthus rushed for eager glory of the game, resolved to get the discus. But it bounded back from off the hard earth, and struck full against your face, O Hyacinthus! Deadly pale the God's face went—as pallid as the boy's. With care he lifted the sad huddled form.

The kind god tries to warm you back to life, and next endeavors to attend your wound, and stay your parting soul with healing herbs. His skill is no advantage, for the wound is past all art of cure. As if someone, when in a garden, breaks off violets, poppies, or lilies hung from golden stems, then drooping they must hang their withered heads, and gaze down towards the earth beneath them; so, the dying boy's face droops, and his bent neck, a burden to itself, falls back upon his shoulder: "You are fallen in your prime, defrauded of your youth, O Hyacinthus!" cries Apollo. "I can see in your sad wound my own guilt, and you are my cause of grief and self-reproach. My own hand gave you death unmerited—I only can be charged with your destruction.—What have I done wrong? Can it be called a fault to play with you? Should loving you be called a fault? And oh, that I might now give up my life for you! Or die with you! But since our destinies prevent us you shall always be with me, and you shall dwell upon my care-filled lips. The lyre struck by my hand, and my true songs will always celebrate you. A new flower you shall arise, with markings on your petals, close imitation of my constant moans: and there shall come another to be linked with this new flower, a valiant hero shall be known by the same marks upon its petals.

—Ovid, *Metamorphoses*, Book 10, translated by Brookes More

I saw you noticed me taking my shirt off. You probably recognize me— you know, from statues? Or the sun. Guilty! It's me. How would you like to have a flower named after you?

—Apollo to Hyacinthus, author's imagination

are you up
if so do you want to play frisbee and die for each other

—Hyacinthus to Apollo, ibid.

In the ninth grade I was very much in love with a boy who wanted to run for class president, so I said that I would help him plan his campaign. We spent an entire Saturday together—almost ten hours— and it was like trying to get the sun's attention. He just kept rotating away while still keeping me warm. First he was hungry, so I offered to make him Eggo waffles, in the hopes that it would make him love me; then he wanted to ride bikes back to his house so he could get the poster boards that he'd forgotten; then there was a Subway sandwich shop we passed on the way back and he was hungry again.

So the day unspooled itself out and made me dizzy; I cooked him waffles and then I pedaled as fast as I could to keep up with him—because he could bike faster than me and did not pay attention when I struggled—then I watched him eat a sandwich, and then I made a poster for him; then we rode our bikes again, and I made him more waffles and more posters, and none of it ever turned into kissing, no matter how many waffles I toasted or blisters I ignored or Subway sandwich bags I carefully wrapped around my handlebars, and he never became student body president, either. Nobody can relax completely while simultaneously demanding someone else's full attention quite like a clear-skinned ninth-grade boy who doesn't know he's going to lose the campaign for student body president yet; nobody is less relaxed than a future trans man toasting every waffle in the house, trying to alchemize Eggos into a kiss. "Chary observation" and "romantic agitation" were the watchwords of that day, and every other day I spent in the kitchen trying to slow a boy down long enough to give him time to kiss me.

The following Sunday I was forced to buy a new box of Eggos for the family out of my allowance, as Eggos were dear and carefully parceled out in our home. I was careful, too, with my attention, my approval, my company, for it was obvious even as a lovestruck fourteen-year-old that boys were too careless of others not to be careful with, but every so often I could not contain my longing to be generous as only a lover is generous, and offer a bridal feast for bewildered Midwestern teenage boys. This meant that I spent a fair portion of my youth watching boys play video games; an invitation from a boy to come over and watch him play video games was considered at the very least to be a real overture toward friendship, and possibly something more. Often, unless one worked very hard to resist it, afternoons spent doing something else entirely sometimes spontaneously turned into afternoons watching boys play video games simply by accident. I'd be at the mall, or trying to get my driver's license, and turn around to find myself on someone else's couch in someone else's basement watching boys watch little representations of themselves on a screen.

It wasn't all sexism, either; often I'd be invited to take a turn and decline, unwilling to let them see my incompetence after their success. I never wanted to play with boys unless I'd already figured out a guaranteed way never to lose, which meant I never played. It was unbearable that they should be so beautiful and allowed to see me at the same time; whenever I became conscious of my own unbearableness I would retreat to the kitchen and talk to whomever I found in there, usually their mothers but sometimes their younger siblings and sometimes no one at all. Either the boys would notice and emerge in search of their audience or they wouldn't and I'd just keep retreating out the front door until I ended up all the way back home. And it was endlessly inane, and frustrating, and the invitations just kept coming, and sometimes the video games were outside and called soccer or Ultimate Frisbee, but it couldn't have really been Ultimate Frisbee because there was always more Frisbee left at the end of it, and I wanted to die, but I was never lucky enough to take a discus to the face and fall into a beautiful boy's arms, so I just kept going home and waiting for something else to happen.

Lord Byron Has a Birthday and Takes His Leave

Oh, well! Fuck you, then,
And I don't have anything else to say about it.
I honestly don't.
I just think it's really, mm, *funny* how—
No, you know what, I honestly don't have anything else
      to say about it.
I really just don't.
Even if you do, I'm just, you know, ZIP, mouth closed, high road.

(By the way, there is a quote from Coleridge that just, mff,
PERFECTLY describes the situation between us and actually just
      your whole deal,
but why bother with it! Why bother, if you're not going to listen
      to me
you're certainly not going to listen to Coleridge.
Which is so funny because it seems like you LOVE listening
      to other people
and all the shit they have to say about me.
But whatever! It's not important, it's really not important to try

to get you to listen to either me or Coleridge about it. Why start
    listening now, right??)

I JUST THINK IT'S REALLY FUNNY!
How someone who's spent so much cumulative time
resting their head against my chest
could end up caring so little about the heart beating just
        underneath it!
It's kind of funny, if you think about it, and I do,
pretty much all the time!

I mean it's fine, obviously,
you don't *have* to treat me well,
no one is going to come and arrest you over it.
You might find a time when life stops being so EASY for you
and you kind of wish you'd stopped being a heartless bitch sooner
(or whenever! I don't know your life).
I don't know, maybe someday you'll get sick of being
so FOCUSED and HARD TO PLEASE and IMPOSSIBLE
        TO READ
and you'll think to yourself, oh my God, you know who had
amazing arms, was Lord Byron. That would be a shame,
if that happened, is all that I'm saying.
I'm not saying that it's *going* to happen.

By the way, I'm moving, so in case anything
gets delivered to the house for me, if I'm not there,
that's why. I'm just telling you this in case some of my mail
shows up and you need to know what to do with it.
I don't know where I'm going to be staying yet.
Probably—honestly, I don't even know, it's impossible to guess.
If you need to forward me my mail, just know that I'm super far away

and you should probably ask one of my friends
one of my many friends—
one of my very many, super loyal friends, many of whom
        live nearby,
because I'm a VERY good friend and they all know what's
        going on with me—
anyhow you can just ask one of them where to forward my mail,
if I get any mail at your house,
which used to be our house but isn't now,
because I'm sure I'll know where I'm staying by then and I'll
definitely be sure to have told one of them by then.
So just ask around.

By the way, and as long as we're on the subject,
you should know that I'm not still mad at you,
even after all the shit you've done to me that I'm not going to
        bother to go into detail over right now because you know
        it and I know it and we are both super clear on the specifics
        of the shit you pulled, so I don't even have to mention it.
I honestly don't have time to go into it all right now.
But you should just know, like for the record,
that I actually still love you,
like a lot, like a really incredible amount,
in a way that says more about the kind of person I am
than the kind of person you are
if you know what I mean.
Ugh, this is already way more than I had time to talk about
        in the first place.
I'm leaving in what is basically the MORNING, tomorrow,
and it's crazy late already, so I'm basically
just wasting time I should be spending packing for my
        amazing new life

in Greece
or, like, wherever I happen to end up
who's to say
whether it's Greece or some other country

(also I just hope you KNOW that if I end up dating a guy after this
it has NOTHING to do with you?? like it is not a STATEMENT
        on you,
please do not read anything into what I do with my life after this
        as a comment on you,
if you happen to see a full-length oil portrait of me and I'm still
        wearing the earrings I stole from you it's not because I'm
        trying to SAY anything so don't overthink this, okay.)
Please feel free to consider us pretty much divorced.
(I know I do!!!)

And feel super free not to even teach our daughter my name.
It would save time, right?
That's all I want for you, is just for you to
have a lot of time on your hands, to really THINK.
About whatever it is that you might need to think about,
anything that your conscience might suggest to you.
I'm not bothered either way, I'm honestly not.

I mean, she might GUESS my name, and if she ends up
        looking like me
(which, objectively, I think we can both agree would be great for her),
IF she ends up looking like me people will probably say something
        about it to her
so she's going to end up learning my name eventually.
I'm not trying to rub anything in, it's just that quantitatively
MOST people know my name, and what I look like,

I don't know if that qualifies as being "famous," just—
most people know about my whole deal, and they're probably
          going to put
two and two together,
so even if you don't teach her my name,
somebody will, and that's not my fault.
If she does end up like me I hope you are a little nicer to her
          than you were to me
but that's not my business!!!!
N O N E of this is my business at alllll, which should be just
          such a relief to you!!!
or who knows,
who honestly knows what you consider a relief!
you're HARD TO READ.

Anyhow, I just wish you the absolute BEST.
I hope SO MANY good things for you, and that
your next boyfriend can figure out how to make you happy,
if that's possible, I sure hope that's possible,
and there's no point in talking about any of the other things
          I could say,
so I won't.
Consider it my last gift to you!
(I've given you *a lot* of gifts, you probably forgot about them.)
Anyhow I'll probably be dead soon,
or at least I can't imagine hurting worse than this!

Anyhow I'm thirty-seven now, I have to, like—oh my God,
thirty-*seven*, and I need to take that really seriously.
No one is even in love with me right now,
which is outrageous (okay, some people are, obviously,
          but none of them count).

What if I'm too old for sex, I'm almost F O R T Y.
Are there even ages you can turn after forty? or do you just
      turn into a tree
oh my God, my body is like autumn,
where all the leaves are falling off the trees
only what's falling off me is hotness

maybe I will just move to Greece
honestly I could just move to Greece and die
and then everyone would want to have sex with me
only it'll be too late
because of how dead and in Greece I'll be
oh my God my life is a mess
I need to just be more like Greece
and then I'll be fine
or dead
or both

This is happening to ME
being thirty-seven and embarrassed is the worst thing I can think of
the hottest thing in the world is not caring
and then being like, seventeen
a seventeen-year-old who's never had a feeling is the only
      acceptable way to live, sexually
and if I'm not careful I'm going to end up being thirty-eight
better just go die in a field
in Greece or wherever, stabbed by some Ottomans
and you can all just live with your own embarrassment when you
      see how dead I am
Okay byyyye, I truly wish you all the best!! ALL OF IT, the
      absolute MOST BEST!

CHAPTER 4

Reasons for Transitioning, in Order

Want to show up good-looking ex

Want to impress good-looking ex

Want to upset good-looking ex

Want to replace good-looking ex

Bored of existing wardrobe, looking for excuse to buy all-new
    clothes that don't fit in a new way

Clothes don't fit/don't feel like driving to store

Younger siblings getting too much attention

Accidentally got accepted into Deep Springs, until recently one of
    the only remaining all-male colleges

Branded advertisement

Neoliberalism??

Want to sing both parts of a duet at karaoke

Important part of upcoming Halloween costume

Empath / "Just a really supportive friend"

Fulfill a prophecy

Nothing good on TV

Too many good shows on TV; feeling overwhelmed and in need
    of a change

Specific codicil in eccentric, wealthy relative's will
Snuck into the Bohemian Grove by accident and needed a
  plausible cover story
Something about upper-body strength
Grabbed the wrong badge at one of those mandatory pronoun-
  name-tag events and felt too embarrassed to admit mistake
Sick of feminist infighting
Intrigued by feminist infighting
Took one of those quizzes, felt obligated
To get more attention from men
Misread brain scan
Forgot about self-acceptance
Thwart a prophecy
Ring finger longer than index finger or something
Excited to reinforce a different set of sexist stereotypes
Cheaper haircuts
Hoping to spearhead a revival of gnosticism
Profoundly misunderstood Freud
Just love layering shirts
Never saw one of those Dove commercials about loving your body
Want to spend more time on the phone with insurance providers
Can't distinguish between good attention and bad attention
Sick of losing at tennis
Forgot that women can be strong
Forgot that men can be sensitive
Deep-seated hatred of chromosomes
Hoping to catch management in a big sexism sting
Got carried away during Breast Cancer Awareness Month
Avoiding something else, like vacuuming

If You Can't Parallel Park, You Have to Get a Sex Change

S omething a lot of people don't know about me is that my transition started the day I failed to parallel park correctly in front of a man standing outside my apartment complex. This is more common than people think! Something like 38 percent of trans men cite the inciting incident of their transition as being watched while failing to parallel park correctly. There's no shame in it, and I wish we made more room for that conversation in our community.

I'd parallel parked in front of my apartment complex hundreds of times at that point. It was, in fact, a point of pride with me at the time that I was a pretty reliable parallel parker, and I'd even volunteered to help a friend struggling to parallel park once or twice in the past by hopping behind the wheel and finishing the job for them. "It's no problem," I'd say, with neither excessive self-regard nor unnecessary self-deprecation. "I'm pretty good at parallel parking."

But something happened this particular day. I don't know if I'd just gotten stuck in my own head, or if the spot I was backing into was a little narrower than usual, or if the curve in the road made the angle more challenging, but I couldn't make it work—halfway into the spot I'd have to admit I was about to run over the curb, or was far closer to the other car's bumper to maneuver any further, and I'd spin the wheel back left and have to pull out into the middle of the street to start again. *Line up your mirrors—get a little closer first—not so close you'll scrape their door—wait until your mirror reaches the middle of the other car to start turning the wheel—*

So I'd had to start over a few times. What of that? It could have happened to anybody. I wasn't sweating yet. I merely turned up the air-conditioning prophylactically. Soon I'd be at home with a nice cup of tea, ready to enjoy the rest of my long and happy life as a woman.

Eventually I noticed a man across the street casually taking in my attempts to park. He wasn't yet watching *me*, you understand, so even at this late point I still held out hope. He was just out scoping the neighborhood, and I happened to be a part of the neighborhood at that particular moment. He wasn't really watching *me* yet. The council would understand if my case came up for review.

A fourth attempt failed. Then a fifth. The man began to take a more specific interest in my parking and wandered over. "It's no problem," I said to myself. "There's no need to panic. You can just drive off and park somewhere else." But I knew, even then, that as soon as he'd seen me, I'd had only two options left to me: park properly, or start transitioning immediately.

When I'd been assigned my particular district as a resident Woman, the local council members had done their best to put me at ease. *We're not looking for reasons to get rid of you*, they said, smiling reassuringly during orientation. *Everybody has the occasional slipup. That's understood around here.* But at my most optimistic I couldn't imagine explaining a nine-time failure *in front of a man over the age of fifty* to the meter maids.

It got worse. The man knocked on my window, and I rolled it down.

"It's a tough spot, huh?" he said cheerfully, and my heart sank in me as I realized he was trying to be nonjudgmental and friendly about the whole thing. He didn't even realize what he was doing.

"Sure is," I bellowed, hoping to mask the quiver in my voice. "I'm having the darnedest time of it!"

"Anything I can do to help?" he asked.

"No, no, I'm fine, thanks," I said. Neither of us believed it.

"You might want to swing a little farther out and try cutting the wheel over a little later," he suggested.

"I'll try that!" I trilled. And I did. What was there to lose at this point? What on earth would the sisters want with a woman who couldn't park her own car on her own street on a sunny day with no time constraints?

So I tried again, this time swinging a little farther out and cutting the wheel over a little later, as the man stood on the sidewalk and called out friendly encouragement. It hardly felt real—I swung the wheel out, then swung it back, all the while trying to remember everything I'd ever heard about transition. I was going to have to buy a whole new wardrobe, and acquire upper-body strength. *While we do think of ourselves as reasonable people,* they'd said at orientation, *obviously we still have limits. And an image to maintain. What we want, of course, is for all of you to be completely successful, and to have all the support you need in maintaining your presence as women in your districts, but within reason. It's one thing to need to circle the block and look for an easier place to park—we've all been there—but if, say, you were to try and fail to parallel park in a place you'd parked hundreds of times before, and you failed ten times in a row, and a man saw you do it—well.*

Has that ever *happened?* someone asked.

Anything can happen, was the only answer. *It's just an example.*

The man got friendlier and more helpful, and I got closer and closer to tears. Eventually I turned back out into the middle of the street and then gunned it, driving as fast as I could until he disappeared from my rearview mirror. I ended up parking on an empty street about a mile away and walking home, all the while knowing what was already waiting for me.

By the time I made it upstairs I found a little vial of testosterone cypionate on the bed, along with a few eighteen- and twenty-two-gauge needles, a pamphlet from a nurse practitioner, a bottle of finasteride, some isopropyl alcohol wipes, and a note that read, simply:

YOU UNDERSTAND, OF COURSE, WE WISH YOU ALL THE BEST IN YOUR FUTURE ENDEAVORS, BUT YOUR SERVICES ARE NO LONGER REQUIRED.

Anyhow, I heard about your trouble parking yesterday and some of the guys sent me over to let you know it happens all the time, and nobody blames you for it. We have a sort of unofficial trans parallel-parking club, as it happens, and if you ever want to join us, we meet in the Safeway parking lot down by the marina most Sunday nights. It's not such a bad life. Most of us have a little trouble with spatial reasoning and splitting the check if there's more than three people at the table, but on the plus side we can park anywhere we want.

CHAPTER 5

Unwanted Coming-Out Disorder

I could not possibly have known I was trans as a child. When my friends and I went through the normal developmental stage of trying to set household items on fire during eighth-grade sleepovers, we always used Bath & Body Works cucumber-melon spray as an accelerant. What could have been more womanly than that? If pressed to think about the subject further, I imagine I might have considered it a net positive for female representation among pubescent firebugs and nascent arsonists. The closest I came to expressing anything remotely along the lines of a desire to transition was trying to open a savings account in the fourth grade under the name "Savannah Hall," and later spelling my given name with one "L" instead of two on all of my seventh-grade home-work assignments. The savings account never took, but Savannah received promotional mailers from the Bank of America well into high school.

I spent the majority of my adolescence longing to be an adult, and the joys of being not-a-child (living independently, leaving mugs in the sink, the freedom to treat my body and possessions with indifference as a response to stress of any kind) have always outweighed the attendant difficulties (bills, aches and pains, los-ing the ability to recover quickly from a sleepless night). Being a

grown-up is a joy that has never lost its shine, so you might imagine my frustration, upon arriving at an understanding of myself
as a transgender adult, to find that the national conversation was
shifting almost immediately—almost as if in direct response—to
questioning the existence of transgender children. It felt rather as
if I had walked into a party and started to introduce myself only
to hear, "I'm sorry, we're looking for someone younger," especially
because I spent no brief amount of time asking myself why I *wasn't*
younger, why I'd spent so much of my life carefully avoiding any
questions about gendered directionality.

I don't pretend that this is a uniquely trans problem, of course; anyone who arrives at their thirties still profoundly self-centered might
feel similarly let down. But the sting remained nevertheless, not
least because I felt personally indicted and shoved into a conversation about children I would greatly have preferred to have about
myself. "But I don't especially want to talk about trans children," I
protested. "I want to talk about *me*. I wish the trans children all the
best, but don't make me share my debutante ball with them."

In August 2018, the following things happened in the following
order: I flew to Dallas to have top surgery, I marked the fifth anni-
versary of my sobriety, and the open-access scientific journal *PLOS
One* published a survey by Lisa Littman about "rapid onset gender
dysphoria," a term coined by a group of parents of trans and questioning children. (I have a constitutional dislike of being upstaged
and felt, quite sensibly, that this was a transparent grab for attention targeted at me personally. Here I was, brand-new chest hot off
the press, still in its original factory packaging, and it was already
old news.) More specifically, the term had been coined by parents
who frequented one of a handful of trans-antagonistic forums like
Transgender Trend and Youth Transcritical Professionals. There

was the expected controversy on publication, of course, not least because the type of parent who posts regularly on a website called Transgender Trend might not be especially inclined to describe their child's coming-out process as particularly balanced or worthy of respect. "Parents describe that the onset of gender dysphoria seemed to occur in the context of belonging to a peer group where one, multiple, or even all the friends have become gender dysphoric and transgender-identified during the same timeframe. Parents also report that their children exhibited an increase in social media/internet use prior to disclosure . . ." Rapid-onset gender dysphoria might more aptly be called, then, "unwanted coming-out disorder," where parents belong to a peer group in which one, multiple, or even all their friends might self-describe as "a pretty open-minded person, most of the time, but don't you think this is taking things a little far?"

The article was eventually updated and republished as what *PLOS One* editor Joerg Heber characterized as a "survey of the parents," rather than a "clinically validated" study, which seems like a fair assessment. Littman herself wrote that "ROGD is not a formal mental health diagnosis at this time," which holds the sort-of-charming implication that it might make it onto 2018's list of *informal* mental health diagnoses, something a busy doctor might offer at the end of a fifteen-minute remote consultation over video conferencing. "I'm sorry I can't offer you something as reassuringly traditional as 'hypertension' or 'gender identity dysphoria,' but we have a ton of ROGD lying around after the last pharmaceutical rep came through the office. If you'd like to take some with you, you're more than welcome to it. Take some for your friends, if you'd like, it's perfectly safe and over-the-counter, and I'd be happy to give you all a diagnosis en masse, if your parents are comfortable with the idea. Now, *at this time*, the diagnosis lacks formality. I'm speaking less as a doctor and more in the style of a slightly officious work acquaintance, or a chatty fellow passenger on a train. Consider this the athleisure-wear of medical opinions: affordable, comfortable, easy to slip into, acceptable at a certain kind of last-minute happy hour, if you don't have time to run home and change into a diagnosis with a fitted waistband."

I was surprised how frequently this came up when I was doing the social transition rounds. I'd come out to a friend, we'd talk broadly about what I'd been contemplating, what I'd been afraid of, what I expected for my future, and after a few minutes, with a mildly pained expression on their face, they'd say something along these lines: "What do you think about those kids who make a lot of trans friends in high school or college, and they're all sort of sad and change their names at the same time? What's that about?" To which I would not usually have much of an answer, since I don't know a lot of teenagers. When pressed ("What are these teenagers doing that you think they ought to be dissuaded or barred from doing? What procedures do you think they have access to? What outcomes do you fear? What futures do you hope for? By the way, do you have a general sense of what hormones do and don't do?"), said friends would rarely be able to point to anything more specific than a vague sense of concern. Lord knows I can relate, having spent plenty of pre-transition time myself letting *I dare not* wait upon *I would*, but I could only muster up meaningful levels of concern for specific situations with concrete details, not the mere idea of some teenager somewhere buying a binder.

It wasn't just that I resented being asked without warning or preparation to furnish some sort of foundational explanation for a sea of vague, hypothetical-sounding trans-adjacent children— although I did, of course—what I *really* resented was that, as freshly minted an out trans person as it was possible to be, I was already old news, swept aside within five minutes of coming out in favor of someone younger, sexier, more complicated. My friends were not interested in my relatively late-in-love, sturdy-thirties transition into a full-grown man. I was being traded in for a younger model. Worse, a *hypothetical* younger model, because no one ever wanted to talk to me about a *specific* possibly trans child, merely the idea that there might someday be a teeming, seething horde of them, bristling with hormones and furious as the forces of hell.

Oddly, the same phrase came up over and over, although I don't think many of these friends had spoken to one another about it: *Something irreversible.* As in, *I'm afraid these kids are going to do something irreversible.* But just what that thing was, and what irreversibility looked like outside of the usual irreversibility of time and momentum, I couldn't have told you, because they were never quite able to explain it to me. "Something irreversible" is to polite people what "self-mutilation" is to impolite people: a quick way to reorient the conversation around their own discomfort with bodies. In both cases it becomes difficult, if not impossible, to have a productive discussion with someone struggling with a reflexive, implicit horror of flesh. Any mention of someone else's transitioning body sends them into direct and panicked conflict with the prospect of their own transitioning body; since this is a prospect they find unbearable, it becomes immediately necessary for them to unload their own desire and disgust onto the nearest suitable target.

For whatever reason, whenever these people—who I believe truly cared for me, who actively willed the good in my life, who wanted to support trans people as much as possible—heard that I was transitioning, their very first, preverbal response was to imagine: *Well, what if someone had forced me to transition?* And whatever their internal response to that question was, usually some combination of horror and relief, would set the tone of the rest of our conversation. In a strange way, I found that rather relatable, since I used to spend a lot of time hoping someone would force me to transition, too, so that I could become a man without having to explain myself or answer any difficult questions. But it quickly snowballed into a rising sense of panic (*Wait a minute. If someone had forced me to transition just because I liked playing with boys' toys when I was nine, I wouldn't have the life I have today. And I like the life I have today! Why are you trying to take my life away from me?*). I'd have to do my best to calmly reason away: "You can keep your life! You're not like me. Someone would have told you if you were like me! You'd definitely know by now if you were like me. Even though I didn't know I was like me until quite recently, and it came as quite a surprise. Oh, no—maybe you *are* like me. Maybe you would never have known that you were like me as long as I'd never told you, but now that I've told you you've started thinking about it, and once you start thinking about it you can't stop, and now you *are* going to have to transition—my God, it *is* contagious! Get everyone else out of this coffee shop, for the love of Christ, if you want to maintain persistent gender continuity—it's onsetting rapidly, this gender dysphoria, and I don't know who it's going to claim next!"

A mother, midforties, presents with the distressing case of her son, thirty; an unremarkable childhood gave way to a bog-standard adolescence and showed every sign of developing into an unexceptional manhood until a wedding at Cana (the influence of out-of-town friends?) then, suddenly and without warning (one odd moment around the age of twelve, if we're being strictly honest, when he had been separated from his parents and other relatives and spent a little unsupervised time talking with teachers in the temple courts, but honestly, nothing since then), full-blown messianic identity disorder, a total change in social groups, all new friends, most of them unattractively dressed, a sudden fixation with fatherliness, miraculous wounds, unexplained twelve-year emissions of blood, unflattering haircuts, unusual new grooming rituals involving feet, hair, and perfume, a tendency to take metaphorical language about abundance, bread, and wine too literally, generally antisocial behavior, etc., etc. Nothing in the child's behavior between the ages of birth and thirty accounts for this abrupt change in demeanor and habit. Further research is required before a formal diagnosis can be made; however, a number of like-minded parents in the area share a growing concern that underlying issues of depression and anxiety may be responsible. Moreover, many of them report that a disproportionate number of their messianically minded children have espoused similarly eschatological worldviews after coming into contact with one another.

Of course there's nothing wrong with trying to understand something a friend is experiencing by imagining, if just temporarily, what it might feel like if it happened to you. The trouble only begins when it triggers an empathy-overload feedback loop and you start to imagine that it's about to happen to you, that any minute now someone is going to travel back to your own adolescence, seize upon the mildest of gender-nonconforming behaviors (*She climbs trees! He doesn't want his hair cut short!*), and drag you kicking and screaming into a forced-transition factory. I never quite knew how to settle that fear in other people, in part because I wasn't sure what they wanted from me more—permission to consider transition if they wanted to, or permission to enjoy not having to transition. Their fear, as best I could understand it, looked something like this: *Had I known transition was possible and available to me at a younger age, I might have been confused into wanting it, because I wouldn't have been able to understand the difference between wanting to wear a dress and wanting to be a girl,* and the underlying implication was *I'm worried you've been confused into transitioning because you forgot the difference between wanting to wear a dress and wanting to be a girl.*

The best reason for transition, as I understand it, is "because I particularly wish it." I had not been in the habit of thinking very hard about my own feelings about my womanhood until the day

I asked myself if I had any opinions about my gendered future. I was more than a little surprised to find that I did! Such a realization set me on a path of mentally revisiting my childhood for clues, in the hopes that it would somehow endorse or dispel what I was experiencing in the present. My childhood was not especially useful to my adulthood, which I found bitterly disappointing. Some things seemed as if they could be interpreted differently in light of what I was currently debating; others—most—didn't. One thing that came as a relief to me was the realization that absent any sort of narrative about biological destiny or the magic of chromosomes, everyone's description of their internal sense of gender, their own sense of themselves as male or female or anything else, always sounded a little ridiculous, always depended on shorthand and substitution. Any attempts to justify or ground said feelings in externalities inevitably resulted in a sort of half-hearted list of hobbies, interests, toy preferences, instinctive reactions to certain forms of dress or speech or address. So this was not a uniquely trans failure of speech, at least, so much as an example of how difficult it is to put any sense of desire or being into words.

I wanted to transition, or at least I wanted to think about transition as an option, that much was clear. Attempting to retroactively extract my childhood for either justification or foreclosure did not leave me with a sense of possibility. What I wanted, what I needed, was to give myself as much freedom as possible to consider what was available to me, what I wanted, what I was willing to risk, to pay careful attention to myself, to say only: *How are you right now? What direction would you like to shuffle in today? What is the next—and only the next—step that you are willing to take?* I had to often remind myself that simply because I had not consciously experienced a desire to transition since I was very young, it did not necessarily follow that this was pure foolishness or a waste of time, a gratuitous bid for attention or distraction. Like my friends, I had to resist the urge to snatch my former-child-self out of the past and demand a permanent account of myself. Like those concerned parents, I had to allow myself a certain degree of fear, uncertainty, and even repulsion as I dealt with a number of feelings, impulses, desires, and ambitions that seemed at one moment totally contiguous with my lifelong understanding of myself and the next moment to be utterly foreign, entirely inexplicable, and—I dare say—of rapid onset.

My gender was stable, foundational, slow-moving, fixed, deep-rooted, intuitive, obvious, recognizable, immediately legible, and straightforward, until it wasn't. I believed, I *hoped*, that any feeling that made its appearance known suddenly and violently would leave in the same way. If I simply sat tight and waited myself out, I would wake up restored to full and grateful cis womanhood any day now, relieved that I hadn't done anything foolish—*something irreversible*—during my days of delusion. The cis self was ordered, sensible, calm, had an unsurprising past and a predictable future, a worthwhile place in the world; the trans self was panicked, adrift, without plan or explanation, Nebuchadnezzar scrabbling in the fields among the beasts. I thought often of the book of Daniel in those days, and the story of Nebuchadnezzar's humiliation before his subjects in chapter 4, promising myself that as long as I held on and resisted transition long enough, I would eventually be restored to myself:

> All this came upon King Nebuchadnezzar. At the end of the twelve months he was walking about the royal palace of Babylon. The king spoke, saying, "Is not this great Babylon, that I have built for a royal dwelling by my mighty power and for the honor of my majesty?"
>
> While the word was still in the king's mouth, a voice fell from heaven: "King Nebuchadnezzar, to you it is spoken: the kingdom has departed from you! And they shall drive you from men, and your dwelling shall be with the beasts of the field. They shall make you eat grass like oxen; and seven times shall pass over you, until

you know that the Most High rules in the kingdom of men, and gives it to whomever He chooses."

That very hour the word was fulfilled concerning Nebuchadnezzar; he was driven from men and ate grass like oxen; his body was wet with the dew of heaven till his hair had grown like eagles' feathers and his nails like birds' claws.

It is worth noting, perhaps, that after his seven-year tenure among the beasts of the field, Nebuchadnezzar's understanding is returned to him, along with his "kingdom, honor, and splendor," that additional majesty is added upon that which he already possessed as the king of Babylon, that he praises God and once again rules over his lost kingdom; namely, that everything he has suffered, everything he has lost, has been *reversible*. His king's body becomes a beast's body, becomes an ox's body, becomes an eagle's body, becomes a king's body again, but a different kind of king's body than he possessed before, because *this* king's body has experienced madness, bestiality, isolation, language-lessness, the dew of heaven, particulation, abandonment, and restoration. It was only when I was able to relinquish the fantasy of *nothing irreversible*, of *uninterrupted cis-ness*, that I could begin to imagine a livable future for myself, a future that did not depend solely on risk management and self-abasement. Ever since I first articulated to myself a certain degree of gender-conflictedness, ever since I openly wondered whether I might have been having some sort of transgender-adjacent experience, the question had remained in my every waking thought. Not always at the forefront, not always obsessively, not even always distressingly, but once the thought had cleared the event horizon of my consciousness, it was never again unthought.

Once I was able to take the question of regret seriously I was finally, *finally* able to start moving ahead, to start telling other people about my internal experience, to start asking questions, to start imagining possibilities, to start exploring my options. Not taking regret seriously in the old punitive sense, as in, *You probably don't really want this, and the worst thing that could possibly happen is to start to transition, change your mind, and then stop, so anything else in the world is a better alternative than transition*, but taking regret seriously in the sense of saying, *If I try it, and I hate it, I'll stop, and I'll grieve what I've changed or lost; I'm prepared to accept the possibility of regret before I begin.* So often, and in so many ways, I tried to act as if I were already regretting something I had not yet given up, asking myself if I wanted to find an immediate transition off-ramp, if I wouldn't like to give up today, if I wouldn't prefer to do something easier and less embarrassing than test-driving a new name at thirty-one years of age. The time for plausible name-changing had come and gone in the seventh grade, and I'd wasted all my transition chips on spelling "Mallory" with a single "L." There was a time and a place for objecting to one's gender, like waiting to interrupt a wedding in a romantic comedy; if I hadn't protested my name or my body or my role in the great order of things when I was first tasked with them, then I certainly had no business trying to do so now.

The problem that a trans person, even the mere *idea* of a trans person, poses is the problem of time. We either speak up too early (*What five-year-old* really *knows what being a boy or being a girl means? Let's give kids a few years before forcing sex and gender on them and let them just be kids, for Chrissakes*) or too late (*I just don't know where this is coming from. . . . I never would have suspected—you're the last person I would have imagined, well, wanting to—*), either trying to delay and deny puberty or demand a mulligan and try to redo it. Rapid-onset gender dysphoria: too trans, too fast, too furious. I don't remember when I first learned that transition was something a person might pursue; I became briefly acquainted with my first trans person at twenty-two, and he struck me as a very nice man with whom I had absolutely nothing in common, such that it never occurred to me that the word "transgender" could possibly include the two of us. I would not meet another out trans person for another seven years. During my career as a woman, no one ever asked me how I understood myself to be one, but if they had, my answer would have been something along the following lines: Trans people are troubled, or make trouble, or feel trouble, and they know something doesn't work right away. I may not be everyone's idea of a good or a compelling or an attractive woman, but everyone around me agrees that that's my job, and that I'm qualified for it, and if I weren't qualified for it, I'd certainly know by now.

At the beginning of my flirtations with the idea of transition, I started to keep a journal in order to prove to myself that I did not actually want to transition. I opened with this:

> Part of what I have sought to do in the wake of this sudden awareness of my own distress (in addition to going to therapy for the first time in years) is to pay careful attention to myself. I love distraction, and loathe a lack of resolution, or feeling sadness, or anger, or anything negative that does not seem immediately fixable. I am, I think, quite sensitive most of the time, so it was rather a shock to me to realize how successfully I had alienated myself from an awareness of how I was doing on a daily basis. So I have been writing a bit more, meditating more, speaking aloud what I am feeling on a daily basis more, even if only to myself but hopefully to friends as time goes on, etcetera.
>
> And this preoccupation popped up almost immediately after that decision to inquire after my own inner state. Perhaps a week after, perhaps a bit earlier, which feels significant. This does not mean I *am* trans, or that my current comprehension of myself is perfect and permanent. This is merely a catalog of present thoughts, desires, understandings, which may shift at any given time, or give way to new understandings, and any of which may

certainly be reconciled with—I don't know, pick your word, I find them all somehow wide of the mark, cis-ness, woman-ness, female-ness, what have you. My present self. I certainly have no desire to become some sort of dour, reserved, hypermasculine, immediately decipherable man.

I also believe that, if I considered it to be truly necessary, I would be willing to pursue certain aspects of transition. I realize I am hedging a great deal and overemphasizing how relaxed and open-minded I am about all this, as if the reason I started keeping this journal was merely to have a really interesting thought experiment about how to be some cool, masculine-ish, gender-nonconforming woman. Which is, to be frank, not how I would describe the last few months. What has been most destabilizing, most attention-grabbing, most calling for pause, has been the insistent, provocative, haunting question: What if you were you, but a boy? Some kind of boy—I'm not sure what kind? I don't wish to be lost in maleness, or to deny some part of my mannerisms or likes or dislikes or vibes or whatever. It feels consistent with me, although I realize that may be hard for those close to me to understand.

I have been, and sort of am, a good woman. I could be, and sort of am, a good man. Neither option is forbidden to me, and I don't believe there is an inherent virtue in, I don't know, "lifelong gender consistency." One is not better or worse than the other, and I don't believe that a shifting sense of identity is wrong, or a sign of unwellness. I do not *have* to do anything I do not want or do not feel ready for.

An entry from the very next day, written in the panic that follows almost any significant disclosure, read:

This feeling cannot possibly do anything but pass away. I have lived thirty years without it. Or at least not with this current understanding of it. There are times I have been fascinated with maleness in a way I interpreted as personal or specific or romantic desire that I think I understand differently now. And yet the prospect of leaving womanhood does not feel especially urgent. I do not feel a strong desire to exit femaleness, but I do feel a profound stirring to pursue or to gravitate toward or to be pulled in by something else. Yet I cannot imagine what sort of life that would look like. What if I changed my mind? What if I looked ridiculous? What if no one understood? What if I made a half-hearted attempt to feint in the direction of a different gender and grew sick at heart and sank back once it proved too difficult? What if I lost my family? What if it did not bring me any greater joy or greater peace, and I continued to feel this strange combination of exhilaration, fear, discomfort, alienation, isolation, and stomachache?

The journal carries on, bouncing back and forth between chipper open-mindedness and histrionics over the impossibility of it all, for eight months before I told another person what I'd been contemplating. I believed that writing these ideas down would help me realize they were impossible at best and pitiable at worst, and that seeing them written on a page would break the spell they had over my mind. I knew well my own desire for distraction, and wanted to give myself no quarter, no room for prevarication when it came to identifying the source, duration, and direction of my transitioning thoughts. And while I dismissed relatively quickly the idea of my childhood as a source of guidance, I returned over and over again to the scriptures of my youth, to ground and locate myself in the stories of transformation that were already familiar to me. Not because I thought I needed religious permission to transition, and not because I thought Christian history was the best source for a trans ontology, but because that history was mine, unalterably and permanently, no matter what I decided to do with my future. God-consciousness, too, is rapid-onset and strikes without warning: "But, beloved, do not forget this one thing, that with the Lord one day is as a thousand years, and a thousand years as one day" (2 Peter 3:8).

The first letter to the Corinthians in the New Testament is attributed to Paul, a man whose life was changed in a single day upon encountering God on the road to Damascus. In the fifteenth chapter he addresses the question of what is to be done with bodies at the resurrection, whether flesh is a problem or an opportunity in the hands of the Lord:

> But someone will say, "How are the dead raised up? And with what body do they come?" Foolish one, what you sow is not made alive unless it dies. And what you sow, you do not sow that body that shall be, but mere grain—perhaps wheat or some other grain. But God gives it a body as He pleases, and to each seed its own body. All flesh is not the same flesh, but there is one kind of flesh of men, another flesh of animals, another of fish, and another of birds.
>
> There are also celestial bodies and terrestrial bodies; but the glory of the celestial is one, and the glory of the terrestrial is another. There is one glory of the sun, another glory of the moon, and another glory of the stars; for one star differs from another star in glory. So also is the resurrection of the dead. The body is sown in corruption, it is raised in incorruption. It is sown in dishonor, it is raised in glory. It is sown in weakness, it is raised in power. It is sown a natural body, it is raised a spiritual body. There is a natural body, and there is a spiritual body. And so it is written, "The first man Adam became a living being." The last Adam became a life-giving spirit.
>
> However, the spiritual is not first, but the natural, and afterward the spiritual. The first man was of the earth, made of dust; the second Man is the Lord from heaven. As was the man of dust, so also are those who are made of dust; and as is the heavenly

Man, so also are those who are heavenly. And as we have borne the image of the man of dust, we shall also bear the image of the heavenly Man.

—1 Cor. 15:35–49

The answer, then, for Paul, is the body-that-is exists always in anticipation of and conversation with the body-that-will-be, that all flesh is not the same flesh but that bodies please God, that death is always followed by growth, that there are many different types of glory, that dishonor may be followed by redemption, that all things spiritual originate in the goodness of the flesh, that our bodies might come to reflect both where we have been and where we are going. As my friend Julian puts it, only half winkingly: "God blessed me by making me transsexual for the same reason God made wheat but not bread and fruit but not wine, so that humanity might share in the act of creation."

"Behold, I tell you a mystery," Paul writes later in that same chapter. "We shall not all sleep, but we shall all be changed—in a moment, in the twinkling of an eye, at the last trumpet. For the trumpet will sound, and the dead will be raised incorruptible, and we shall be changed."

I never did manage to sort out whether "this feeling," this trans-ness, this transition, is likely to pass away. I have been a mystery, and I have been changed, and I have been first natural and afterward spiritual and borne the images of more than one man. Sometimes in a moment, sometimes in the twinkling of an eye, sometimes quickly, sometimes slowly, sometimes where a thousand years were as a day, and sometimes where a day was as a thousand years.

CHAPTER 6

The Stages of Not Going on T

Oh, I don't want to go on T. That's not what this is. I can see where you got the idea, I suppose, but I'm afraid hormones simply aren't for me. I don't even want the ones I have! I'll never go on testosterone, but it's simply wonderful for you. You look great. Better than ever, honestly. If I were stuck in a room for the rest of my life and could only look at one thing for some reason, it would be you (I hope that's not weird to say), but that's really not the same thing. I just want you to go on hormones and for me to be able to watch you do it. And if you ever wanted to share the occasional update, like just a few day-by-day updates on how you're doing, maybe just a daily journal about what T is doing for you, what affects you're noticing, that sort of thing, that I could read or watch or otherwise follow along from the comfort of home, where I'm not on hormones, that would be ideal. But that's it for me!

I'm not even sure I *want* hormones. I'm pretty sure I don't want them, because I think about going on hormones all the time, and those thoughts always end on some variation of "I can't, not ever," and if I really wanted to try hormones obviously I wouldn't keep thinking about how I can't try them. I think about them all the time and have to constantly stop myself, so I must really not want them. You know how when you're profoundly curious and sick with longing about something, it usually passes pretty quickly. It's an idle fixation brought on by boredom, easily confused with legitimate desire. Don't worry, lots of people confuse the two. And it doesn't help, seeing all those attractively powerful trans people getting into their stretch limousines and then going on the news to promote hormone therapy as a universal panacea for solving all your problems. Happens all the time, and frankly I'm sick of it.

I certainly don't need hormones. See, I've got all these coping strategies instead. Look at how well they're working!

If someone were to drop a little bit of leftover testosterone on the ground, and I couldn't find the owner and there weren't any trans people around, and it was about to go bad, I would probably take it, in the interest of preventing waste. That would just be sensible. Stand to reason. If for some reason I were *forced* to take testosterone—I don't know why someone would be forced, but it might happen—I would of course make the best of a bad situation and comply with good cheer. There's no point in complaining when someone comes to your house and forces you to take testosterone. I'd be remarkably sanguine about the whole thing, a model of radical acceptance. These things happen sometimes, for any number of reasons. One reads about it. Yes, I'm quite prepared to be forced to take hormones, if it ever comes to that, but I wouldn't go out of my way for it.

Oh God, hormones would ruin my *life*. I'm sorry, I don't mean to sound dramatic, but hormones would ruin my life dramatically. Obviously they're great for other people. I think everyone should get the chance to try going on hormones, except for me. I'm the only person who shouldn't take hormones. God, can you imagine? Me? On *hormones*? I imagine it all the time, and I know it would be terrible. No, I've given it a lot of thought and I know that testosterone therapy would destroy all my personal relationships, ruin my sex life, devastate my plans for the future, render me permanently unhappy, and otherwise set off a series of unmitigated disasters that I would regret for the rest of my days. But you look great. I'm perfectly contented as I am—not needing hormones, certainly not wanting them, prepared to take them cheerfully under duress, planning ahead for said duress, secure in the knowledge that they would ruin my life and that I've never wanted them for even a moment.

I definitely don't want to go on T, and I really don't think I've ever even wanted to try hormones, and they would absolutely ruin my life—I know that for sure—but I do wish I'd known about this when I was seventeen. Hormones would ruin my life, but if I'd been able to try them fifteen years ago, I'd be the happiest person in the world. Hormones stood me up for senior prom, and I never really got over it, and I wouldn't give testosterone a second chance if it rang my doorbell right now, begging my forgiveness and asking if we can start over. The fault lies with hormone replacement therapy for not making itself known to me sooner, and it's only fair that I should punish hormone replacement therapy for ignoring me by ignoring it in return.

If I'd known about them even a day sooner, everything would be different; unfortunately I learned about hormones the day after taking hormones became impossible, and you can't blame anyone for that. Timing is crucial. It's simple math, really: only trans people take hormones, and I'm not trans, because trans people are on hormones, and I'm not on hormones, so if I were to go on hormones it would likely cause some sort of paradox. Many other people would be very distressed with me if I *were* to try testosterone, but as long as I don't try testosterone, only I have to be distressed about it, and one is certainly fewer than many, so there's your answer right there. It's simple math.

Of course if I had it to do all over again, I'd take them. Who wouldn't? It would be the best thing imaginable for me. The trick is not to imagine it and not to want anything.

Oh Lacanian Philosopher
We Love You Get Up

The Lacanian Philosopher has gotten a haircut!
He walked into a barbershop
without making an appointment
and sat in the first empty chair
and said to no one and everyone,
"Cut my hair, make it look awful,
do not look me in the eyes,"
and my mother always said *being a Marxist*
is no excuse
for not looking your best
and what I want to know is what are you really angry at,
capitalism or scissors,
and while I'm at it I also want to know
why it is I keep mixing up Ted Hughes and Frank O'Hara
when poor Frank never did a thing to Sylvia
but that haircut is devoid of integrity
and propped up on a faltering infrastructure
and would it kill you to smile
or take a shower and get some rest

you can give primacy to the discourse-manipulating creative subject
and still use a comb, you know
because your friends are worried about you
your friends and your mother are worried about you
your friends are worried about you and your hair
your friends are worried about you and your hair and your views
　　　on subjectivity
oh Lacanian Philosopher we love you get up
and stay out of Fire Island.

CHAPTER 7

The Several Mortes D'Arthur
(Kindly do not remember the last
name of Sir Thomas Malory)

*How King Arthur Begged a Friend to Cast the Sword Excalibur
into the Water, and How He Was Tendered Over to a Boat Full of
Ladies; in Short, How He Died*

There are three stages to dying. (My heart works so, to tell you
this story.) The first is to lay down your arms and give your sword
back to the lake that gave it to you in the first place. The next is
to step into a river. Then all the women you have ever known,
including the woman who hated you most in life, arrive on a boat
and bear you away to an island. Where the boat goes after that, no
one knows. Perhaps the women go on a cruise. They have a lot in
common besides you, and quite possibly a great deal to talk about,
after all.

Only they who can describe what they bear are worthy to carry
arms, or put them down again. After a long day's fighting, and a
great many wounds, the king decided to fall to the ground and
perish. Then Sir Lucan of the royal household lifted his body up
to bear him away. In the lifting of his king's body did Sir Lucan of

the royal household perish. In the lifting the king swooned, and in the catching Sir Lucan swooned himself, and in the swoon an old wound reopened that the guts of Sir Lucan fell out of his body and therewith his heart burst. Was it fair for such a true knight to die so? Thus when the king awoke from his swoon he saw Sir Lucan run aground, foam at his lips and his guts spilled out at his feet. Alas, the king said, that the good Sir Lucan should have his death so, and death at my feet, when he would have helped me when he had more need of help than I. So everyone around him swooned once more for good measure.

If I were dying slower, the king said, we might still weep awhile, but the time is sped, and the boat approaches, and I have still got my sword Excalibur, which is no fit tool to meet death with. Someone throw this in the lake for me—unless you too have any secret injuries you are hiding from the rest of us, that might make you expire nobly in the performance of your duties. And either Griflet or Bedivere threw it in the lake.

Is Excalibur truly gone? asked the king. Not hidden in the reeds or anything? And either Griflet or Bedivere avoided his eyes, and said, Definitely, with its long and gleaming blade and rich pommel overstudded with precious stones, back to the lake and the women who forged it there.

What saw you there? asked the king.

I saw the wind, and the waves, and the good sword Excalibur sinking beneath them, nothing more.

Then the king turned his face from them and said, Friend, you lie to me. As you love me, go back and give my sword to the water, and do not covet it, but come back and tell me what you see.

Fine, said either Griflet or Bedivere.

That was awfully fast, said the king. I fear me greatly to die with my sword near me.

I don't know what to tell you, said either Griflet or Bedivere—it is not recorded which—I took up the sword and girded it, and hove it into the water, where it was met by a hand that emerged from the water, and brandished it thrice, before disappearing with the long and gleaming blade, and the rich pommel, and all the precious stones studded thereupon. But it all happened very quickly.

Have we tarried? the king asked them over again and over. Have we tarried overlong? I dread me we have, and tomorrow you will find me dead where I lie. Here come the ladies, here come the ladies, say good night to all the ladies, fellows. At Pentecost the Spirit visits all flesh; be prepared for it.

At the water's edge hoved a little barge with many fair ladies in it, and among them no mean number of queens, and they all bore about their heads black hoods, and wept and shrieked at the sight of King Arthur, who was borne among them and set him down in one of the lady's laps. And then the greatest queen among them said: Ah, dear brother, why have ye tarried so long from me? Alas, this wound on your head has caught over-much cold.

And the king said, That is exactly what I told them, back on the shore.

You were right, said his sister.

Thank you, the king said, and beyond that no man on shore heard what he said thereafter, for the boat sped itself speedily downriver and was soon lost to sight and speech.

So everyone took in that what comfort they could, except for Sir Lucan, who lay still on the shore with foam at his mouth and his guts at his feet. He died without the witness of women, and without water, and with his sword still strapped to his side, which can't mean anything good for Sir Lucan.

Alternatively: How King Arthur Pleaded with His Good Friend Sir Bedivere to Help Him Die Drunk

"Leave off the arguments, please," begged King Arthur. He tried to scoot his back up such that he could prop himself up on his elbows, failed, and gave it up as a bad job. "There isn't time, not with a boat full of my sisters flying down the river, and this soul-wound looking to speed me fast. I'm simply asking you to listen. *Agree or disagree*: encountering death with one's full faculties intact is a horrific prospect, all other things being equal."

"Agree," said Bedivere.

"Agree," Arthur continued, "one cannot help being mortal. Although if a third exception in history is ever to be made, likely as not it will be made in my case."

"Third exception? What were the first two?"

"Enoch and Elijah, ass. Ascended to Heaven without dying. Chariots of fire, and so on, cf . . . cf something. Book of Kings."

"What about—what about the other one?"

"*Christ* doesn't count."

"No, the other one. With the sisters."

"Lazarus?"

"Lazarus."

A pause. "Doesn't count," Arthur concluded triumphantly. "It was only a postponement, not a commutation of sentence. Doesn't count."

"Has to count for something."

"Doesn't count for this."

"It doesn't say he dies again, does it? No word of him dying again. He could have been the third."

"It doesn't have to say he died again. It's a given, dying."

"Awful lot of givens in your argument."

"Giving Lazarus a miss at this stage—" Arthur began.

"I don't see how you can give Lazarus a miss," Bedivere said.

"Are you suggesting that Lazarus is still walking among us?"

"Just don't see how you can give Lazarus a miss."

"Giving Lazarus a miss," Arthur said, "and barring the possibility of exception (which there's no sign of, I think we can both agree; look at poor Sir Lucan the foamy), the only aspect of the present situation I can control are my faculties. If one has to die, one had better die drunk, so as not to be so bothered by it. And since the hour is not known to any, not even the Son of Man, best to be as drunk as possible as often as possible, to improve one's chances. And since the hour is looking awfully imminent at this point, there's no harm in fortifying oneself against the likeliest possibility. And since I can't get any for myself at present"—here he briefly looked down at himself and cursed—"you've got to be a dear and get something to drink for me."

"But I haven't got any money on me," Bedivere said dazedly.

"You have my good sword Excalibur," the king said, "that noble sword whereof the pommel and the haft are all of precious stones; take that rich sword and get me with drink from it. Bedivere, please. Bedivere, Bedivere, Bedivere, please, Bedivere, get me with drink. The boat cometh, and I am not prepared to board it. This is the last, the last, the last chance. Even if hurt comes from it, it will be the last hurt, and you can acquit yourself of guilt from it."

So Sir Bedivere departed from him, although he was loath to do it, and by the way he thought of his noble king, and said to himself: *If I throw this rich sword into the water, and tell the king there was no drink to be found, thereof shall come no harm, but only good, for I have seen the king when he gives himself over to drink, and I will not put him to drink again by my hand.* So he hurled Excalibur into the lake, and a hand came up out of the water and grasped the sword, and shook it fiercely three times before vanishing itself back under the waves.

Therefore Sir Bedivere returned and said to the king that there was no drink to be had, not even for something as dear as the sword Excalibur.

That were untruly done of you, my darling, the king said.

It were truly meant, Bedivere said.

As you love me, said the king, do my bidding; as you love me, keep your word; as you love me, bring me the last drink, oh please.

Then Sir Bedivere went away again, and thought it sin and shame to let the king end in drink instead of glory, and so he did not come back at all. King Arthur lay a-waiting, and never did he see Bedivere again. This long tarrying putteth me in great danger of my life, Bedivere, he cried out. But if thou do now as I bid thee, if ever I may see thee again, I shall slay thee with mine own hands, for thou wouldst for my rich sword see me dead!

But Bedivere was a true friend to him, and stayed away. And King Arthur lay in the dirt and cursed his friend's name until he died.

Alternatively: How King Arthur Curled His Arms and Legs Around His Body Like a Starfish and Recited H. G. Wells to Himself in Panic and Heart's Terror

"Not to go on all fours. The lump of mystery opposite is a man, a five-man," the king gabbled to himself. "He comes to live with us. The pause is interrogative; he comes to live with us, he comes to live with us and learn the Law. Stay a while, Bedivere; are we not men? Say the words, Bedivere, before the lump of mystery comes to live with us. If Bedivere will not say the words, Lucan might, if Lucan lives. Not to go on all fours, that is the law, not to suck up drink, that is the law, not to chase other men, that is the law. Are we not men? Does the boat approach, Bedivere? I don't want to be king again, no matter how great the need or dark the hour. Don't make any promises on my headstone, Bedivere; I make you no promises now. Are we not men? God, why won't any of you touch me, or hold my hand?"

Alternatively: How Everyone Was Impaled with Spears and the Fisher King Was More Than a Little Irritated by It

Here is a list of all the men who were braken on one another's spears that day: Sir Gonereys, Sir Palomides in disguise, Semound the Valiant, Meliagaunce, King Bagdemagus and King Marsil of Pomitain, Sir Breuse, Sir Galahalt, Sir Lamorak, Sir Corsabrin, Sir Ossaise of Surluse, the Earl Lambaile, the King of Northgalis and the Earl Ulbawes, Sir Gawaine, Sir Tristram, Galihodin, Sir Uwaine, Sir Lucanere, Sir Bliant, Sir Bors, and Sir Sagramore. And the Fisher King, with his vague and suppurating wound somewhere between his heart and his feet, had them all born inside his castle Corbenic on litters, and saw to it that all the wounded were attended with all care and courtesy, but his heart within him grumbled, and he snuck himself away from their sickbeds to sit beside the bleeding lance awhile. His had been the wound first, after all.

Alternatively: How King Arthur Snuck Away from the Field of Battle and Lived with Guinevere as Faithful Nuns in Almesbury, Sweet and Loving Sisters Who Were Buried One Beside the Other, Underneath the Same Headstone

(Upon such sacrifices the gods themselves throw incense.) When Queen Guinevere came to know that King Arthur was slain and many a noble knight beside, she stole away to Almesbury and made herself a nun, wearing white clothes and black, and did a great penance, as great a penance as the meanest sinner ever took. All manner of people marveled at how greatly she was changed, and now an abbess.

And Arthur stole away from Avalon in white clothes and black, too, and whispered at Guinevere's window: What, alive, sweet girl? Come, let's away together, we two alone will sing like birds and sisters; you kneeling and asking blessing, me kneeling and asking forgiveness, spies of God and live a secret, wearing out the walls and prisons and lives of great ones, in sweet repentance, but come away from that window there, love!

And Guinevere laughed! and opened her window! and they lived in sweetest charity ever after!

Alternatively: How King Arthur Hardly Felt It at All

"It doesn't feel like anything," he said, "and I really do think this is it. It hardly feels like anything at all, and I'm sure that this is the real thing."

Cosmopolitan Magazine Cover Stories for Bewildered Future Trans Men Living in the Greater Chicago Area Between the Years 1994–2002

Cosmopolitan *Magazine:*
Don't Bother Asking Anyone Else About It,
Just Assume Most Women Feel This Way

"I Just Happen to Be a Modest Person—But *You* Look Great In It!" and Other Demurrals

Breasts and Your Summer Wardrobe: Other People Seem to Like That You Have Them, Just Take Their Cues and Go From There

Nobody Likes Fitting-Room Mirrors, So Don't Waste Time Investigating Your Own Fitting-Room Experiences: Most Women Have Negative Body-Image Issues, So It's Safe to Say That's Probably Just What You're Feeling, Too

Try the Pill: It's Still HRT, Kind Of

Dress for Success: Getting Male Attention with the Body You Have, Not the Body You Want

We Polled 100 Readers About Sex: "Mostly This Seems Fine."

If You're a Boy, Then Why Are All the Boys *You* Know Either Mean or Indifferent Toward You? Checkmate.

How to Half-Heartedly Try to Dress Butch Once and Look Weird So You Never Think About *Waves Arms Generally* That Whole Thing Again

Fan Fiction: Maybe That's What This Thing Is? I Don't Know, You're Not Giving Me a Lot to Work With Here

Maybe Try That Microwaved Doughnut Trick? Anything to Keep Attention Off Whatever Your Body's Doing Right Now

If You Were, You'd Know, and You Don't Know, So You're Not. Right? Do You Know? Does Someone Else Here Know? And Other Letters to the Editor (She Doesn't Know, Either, Please Stop Writing and Asking)

Marcus Aurelius Prepares for the New Year

I just want to start by acknowledging some of the people who got me here: from Diognetus, who kept me away from quails; to my mother, who kept me away from the idle rich; to my great-grandfather, for keeping us rich enough so none of us had to go to public school so we could really focus on what we wanted to do with our own money without picking up bad habits from other rich people. Does that sound braggy? I'm sorry if it does; I honestly don't mean it that way. But also, *how* does a person work on a gratitude list without sounding braggy, unless they want to pretend they're not grateful for the things they're actually grateful for?

Hoo. It's—hoo, boy. Just focus on one thing. Just focus on the thing ahead of you.

I know it's kind of hokey, but honestly, after the year this year has been, maybe I could use a little hokey, you know? It's not like anything else has worked. It's sort of like—I, emperor of Rome, son of Marcus Annius Verus, heir to Hadrian, *know*, on some level, that just going to bed earlier and drinking more water isn't magically going to fix everything, that eventually when it comes to bedtimes and water a person is going to start to experience diminishing returns, and that it's not going to suddenly solve all my problems and make me the sort of person who gets cheerfully out of bed at *gallicinium*, ready to face the sunrise. But it's also like, okay, there's not a lot that's within my control right now, *and* that's good for me, *and* that's free, *and* that I can do throughout the day as a reminder to look after myself, you know? So fuck it, yes, I'm going to try to drink more water this year, and I'm not going to be embarrassed about it.

Starting this year, I'm not going to be surprised when people disappoint me anymore. This sounds defensive, but I don't mean it in, okay, a pointed way, I swear. I think of my father, and how he released his friends from all obligation to get dinner with him when he was in town, no matter how far he had traveled to see them and honestly I would love to be just in that same place emotionally. *If you can make it, amazing. If not, I totally get it.* And I would love to get it!! There will *be* other dinners. (And if not, so much the better; it's a chance to prepare for the final and ultimate dinnerlessness.)

I'm just going to wake up—*WHENEVER* I wake up, and I'm not going to beat myself up if I oversleep once in a while; that's just a sign that my body probably needs the rest, right?—and say to myself, okay, some people today are probably going to be really *challenging*, because they haven't found a way yet to stand in the light, and it's not that they're trying to make my life more difficult, they just don't Get It Yet.

Not that I'm trying to say that I *get it*! Ahh! Good thing no one's ever going to see this, idk idk idk, I just mean I'm going to try to respond with patience, and to remember that no one can ever make me feel small without my permission. Or participation; maybe "permission" is too shame-y toward myself. Because if we're *all* part of the same divine material, it's not even possible for someone else to hurt me, which is why it doesn't even make sense for me to still carry around dark energy w/r/t Antoninus. I want to release that energy! I really do! And if I want to do it, then I do it! Antoninus,

I release that energy toward you; I mean, I imagine it was probably really hard for him to see me become quaestor before I was even twenty-four! I would definitely feel raw about if the situations were reversed.

Not that I want to spend time trying to read other people's minds in the new year. I'm just: I release it. It's honestly not my business if Antoninus or Gracchus or whomever is jealous of me, if they even are jealous of me. I don't even want to know if other people are jealous of me. I want to spend more time this year *releasing* things, whether that's just clutter around the house or relationships that don't honor the higher self or books I'm never going to get around to reading, because I really want to get in touch with my own mortality. Not that I want to spend a lot of time obsessing over death, because I can't change it, but I want to live in a constant state of radical acceptance so that when I *do* die it's not like *Oh my God, ahh, death!!! like, DEATH!!!* but more like, *Yes, okay, this.* Does that make sense??

Because if I'm really just honest with *myself* right now, I can accept that I'm never going to read all of these books. I keep buying them and *saying* I'm going to read them, and then I don't. Then when people say things like, "Oh, Marcus, what are you reading right now?" which is a perfectly innocent question, I feel like they're trying to GET me, and I'll just name whatever books I recently bought (which, is that compulsive?? Need some time to sit with THAT question later) and hope they don't ask any follow-up questions because then I have to guess what I think the book is probably about (not that a book can really be ABOUT anything lol) and that kind of feels like lying. So I usually just end up saying something like "Oh, actually I'm rereading _____ right now," and then I just name a book I've read before even though I'm not rereading it right now, just in case the secret underlying question was "Have you ever read a book?"

Relatedly!! I don't want to keep PUTTING EVERYTHING OFF. I sometimes feel like I just say yes to everything because I don't want to disappoint anybody, and then I can't do everything, because I'm *human*, and then I *do* end up disappointing people, and maybe it's better to just say no more often, and to accept that I'm not always going to be able to get back to everyone about everything, and that sometimes I actually NEED to do NOTHING because I'm a person, not a job. I'm going to treat time like a resource this year, instead of a problem to be solved.

And to that end, I want to be really mindful about how much coffee I drink this year! More water, less coffee! Coffee just makes me jittery and anxious, not wakeful, and Theophrastus always says that it's worse to fuck up when you're jittery than when you're just consciously like, *Yes, I want to do this thing that may not be right for me right now except for maybe that's what makes this thing right for me right now*, and I really want to be more like Theophrastus in a lot of ways, while also still being myself.

I want to spend less time worrying this year about what people think about me, and to let go of the delusion that people even *are* thinking about me, because maybe they aren't! I mean yes, okay, I still have my *job*, I know that people have to think about the emperor of Rome sometimes for *work*, but that doesn't define me, and honestly someday there's going to be an emperor of Rome who *isn't* me, like Pontius Laelianus's son or Commodus or Titus or whomever. God, that's weird to think about. But this is the year I stop allowing other people to take the present moment from me, which is my only possession, which is why I think I'm finally ready to get rid of all my furniture, like the Cynic Monimus. Maybe a cot, as a sort of gesture, that I won't actually sleep on.

So not that these are *formal resolutions* or anything, because I don't want to set myself up to "fail" or "succeed" at something before the year has even started, because this is the year when I stop setting impossible goals for myself that go against my own nature; this is the year I really try to meet myself where I'm already *at* and maybe just bring myself a cup of water and a sense of acceptance. I'm just recording my thoughts without judgment.

The soul of man does violence to itself FIRST OF ALL WHEN I get angry or irritated at someone else and forget that we are all part of the same nature. So it's not actually possible for someone to "cut me off" or "interrupt me," so there's no point in getting angry over it. That doesn't mean I'm not allowed to get angry! It means I'm releasing the *delusion* that anger is a *possibility* in those moments.

The soul of man does violence, etc. SECOND OF ALL WHEN I turn away from any other fellow creature, or move toward anyone with the intention of anger. So, like, why would I even eat dairy anymore? It's not a *rule* I have to follow; I'm not like, officially "not eating dairy anymore" if anyone asks, I'm just going to ask myself in the moment, *Am I moving toward a fellow creature in acceptance or in an attempt to dominate?* And make my decision from there. Which means I probably just won't even eat dairy anymore, but it's not like it's going to be a big deal. I'll just ask myself more questions before I impulsively reach for cheese, and everything will fall into place after that.

And the soul of man does violence to itself THIRDLY WHEN I get overwhelmed by either pleasure or pain. That doesn't mean I'm not allowed to feel things!

The FOURTHSOME way the soul of man does violence to itself is when it acts or speaks insincerely/untruly. So if I haven't read a book and someone asks about it, I'm just going to speak the truth: "I haven't read it, actually." I'm not even going to say, "I haven't read it yet," to try to have it both ways because I don't know if I ever will, and this is the year I stop trying to claim intention as certainty. Ahh! This is like . . . exciting, actually. Obviously I know it's a lot to ask of myself but I really think I'm ready to start stepping into these habits this year.

And FIFTH OF ALL, soul-violence happens when said soul allows any act of its own and any movement to be without an aim, or does anything thoughtlessly and without considering what it *is*, it being right that even the smallest things be done with reference to an end; and the end of rational animals is to follow the reason and the law of the most ancient city and polity. So like: I have *handled* the Costoboci and the Christians and Avidius Cassius of Syria, and I don't have to keep worrying about them once I've achieved my goals. I'm leaving them all in the last year.

And then this part doesn't really fit into a list or anything, but I wanted to include it here: Of human life the time is a *point*, and the substance is in a *flux*, and the perception dull, and the composition of the whole body subject to putrefaction, and the soul a whirl, and fortune hard to divine, and fame a thing devoid of judgment. So it's not really a Good or a Bad thing that I personally am extremely famous, and I need to just exist in a neutral space w/r/t my being a famous person. It's a stream and a dream and a sojourn and oblivion and there's just a big river that we all belong to.

So: what's left, if I choose to release (sorry, if I *choose* to *acknowledge* that I have *already* released) those things? Philosophy! And it's that energy, that mind-spirit, that gods-consciousness that can keep me from violence, separated from both pain and pleasure, hold me to my purpose, not worrying about what Avidius Cassius is doing or what Martius Verus is doing but what *Marcus Aurelius* is doing, accepting everything that happens as coming from the same source that I myself come from, whatever that is, and waiting for death with a cheerful but not overeager mind and not compulsively buying more books to distract myself or keeping track of what Galicians actually make time to sit down and have dinner with me when I'm in town (even if I told them weeks in advance and never heard back).

Because even if I quit my job tomorrow and just started reading full-time, there's no way I would ever finish! I have bought my last book. I accept that. I'm not even going to try to guess which was the last book I bought, or worry about whether it's the sort of book I would have chosen as the Last Book to Buy if I'd thought about it in advance. So if death is just a dissolution of the elements that every living being is made of, and elements are always changing, why should I be afraid to change again? That's like being afraid of Tuesday because yesterday was Monday. That's just *life*, and *nature*, and nothing is evil that is in harmony with life, so it straight up does not matter whether Matidia's will has anything in it for me or not, or how heavy the denarius is or isn't, or whatever. Even if I never read another book, I'm still a person with intrinsic value, and later I'll be a river.

This in Carnuntum. Anyway, I'm probably going to delete this later.

CHAPTER 8

Evelyn Waugh and the Opposite of Communion

> For everyone who asks receives, and he who seeks finds, and to him who knocks it will be opened. If a son asks for bread from any father among you, will he give him a stone? Or if he asks for a fish, will he give him a serpent instead? Or if he asks for an egg, will he offer him a scorpion? If you then, being but men, know how to give good gifts to your children, how much more will your heavenly Father give the Holy Spirit to those who ask Him!
>
> —Luke 11:10–13

Evelyn Waugh's eldest son, Auberon, once told the following story about his father in his autobiography, *Will This Do?*: Just after the end of World War II, Evelyn's wife managed to get her hand on three bananas despite fresh fruit being nigh unavailable.

> Neither I, my sister Teresa, nor my sister Margaret had ever eaten a banana throughout the war . . . but we had heard all about them as the most delicious taste in the world. . . . The great day arrived when my mother came home with three bananas. All three were put on my father's plate, and before the anguished eyes of his children, he poured on cream, which was almost unprocurable, and

sugar, which was heavily rationed, and ate all three. A child's sense of justice may be defective in many respects, and egocentric at the best of times, but it is no less intense for either. By any standards, he had done wrong. It would be absurd to say that I never forgave him, but he was permanently marked down in my estimation from that moment.

I think of this story often, which seems over-the-top even for Evelyn Waugh, and how unpleasant the dish must have seemed by at least the second bite: a sort of raw bananas Foster, the sugar grainy and undissolved, the cream slopping everywhere, the sheer size of the thing, the unrelenting monotony of a mouthful of wet banana. The story has everything: joyless dessert-eating, public enforcement of family discipline, excess without taste, banana peels, the showiness of hoarding pleasure. Sad English childhoods always sound like caricatures of themselves, yet they're somehow all true. It doesn't matter if the inheritance is tasteless and unappetizing; a child knows his rights and objects to watching a tasteless banana that is rightfully *his* go to his father all the same. "If a brother or a sister is naked and without food and one of you says to them, Depart in peace, be warmed and filled, but do not give them the things which are needed for the body, what does it profit them? Thus also faith by itself, if it does not have works, is dead" (James 2:15–17). A child might not know what a banana tastes like, and a child might suffer for the longing of it just the same.

COMMUNION: Take bread, and bless it, and break it, and give it to the disciples.

ANTI-COMMUNION: Take bananas, and peel them, and stack them, and hoard them.

COMMUNION: Say, *Take, eat, this is my body.*

ANTI-COMMUNION: Find the most unprocurable cream. Find the most heavily rationed sugar. Commit the act of *pouring* in a stinting age.

COMMUNION: Take a cup, and give thanks, and give it to the disciples.

ANTI-COMMUNION: Take a bite. Swallow a wince at the flavor of soft and spreading banana undercut by milkfat and the sharp grains of sugar. Maintain eye contact with your children as you do.

COMMUNION: Say, *Drink, you, all of it, for this is my blood shed for the remission of your sins.*

ANTI-COMMUNION: Point out the obvious about the banana. Point out what the banana does and does not represent.

COMMUNION: Say to them also, *I will not drink from now on of the fruit of this vine until that day when I drink it new with you in my Father's kingdom.*

ANTI-COMMUNION: Remember that you are eating three bananas swimming in cream on a plate. The odds that some of the cream has run out onto the table and even onto your lap are high, possibly inevitable. Continue the heavy work of chewing and swallowing. This is a meal that can only ever happen once, but reenacted a thousand times in memory.

There are meals that require repetition and there are meals that cannot bear it. And of course you have to know that you are hungry before you can ask your father for bread. But it's not enough to know that you are hungry; you also have to know that others have hungered before you and found the common solution named bread, and that bread is plentiful and readily available for you, that bread is digestible and wholesome and a ready answer to hunger; you have to know what *hunger* is, and what *bread* is and the difference between a loaf of bread and a rock that is shaped like a loaf of bread, though they may look and feel the same in the hand.

You must be able to imagine your own father hungering. Let us further imagine that your father has only ever hungered and thirsted after righteousness, see Matthew 5:6, and has no concept of bread hunger, in which case you have to learn the language of bread and explain it to him, and hope he will be able to compare it to his own hungers. You must trust that your father can tell the difference between a loaf of bread and a stone. You must trust that your father will not say, *Depart in peace, be well and filled*, but does not give you the things that are needed for the body. There are many conditions to be met before anyone might ask and hope to receive.

Now at the start of his ministry Christ was led into the wilderness by the Spirit where he met the devil, and in those days he ate nothing. For forty days he was led by the Spirit and met the devil and ate nothing and went about in the wilderness, so afterward he was hungry. At this same time was his Father in heaven, where they neither hunger nor thirst, nor does the sun strike them nor any scorching heat. And the devil said to him, "If you are the Son of God, command this stone to become bread," by doing so inviting the son to play the father and to give himself his own inheritance; by doing so inviting him to name the terms of his own hunger; by doing so inviting him to take a selfish meal that did not concern itself with the hunger of others or the needment of their bodies. At which Christ referred to Deuteronomy: *God humbled you and caused you to hunger, then fed you with manna which you did not know*

nor did your fathers know, that He might make you know that man
shall not live on bread alone, but by every word that proceeds from the
mouth of the Lord. To which the devil had no answer.

The order of operations, then, is this: In order to hunger, you
must be beloved of God and in need of humility. If you hunger, it is
for the purpose of being fed. What you eat is beyond your knowledge and your father's knowledge. The purpose of food is to sustain
and increase the love of God, whatever your earthly father eats or
declines to eat in front of us. I first began to be a man when I asked
myself why it was that I was not a man; I first knew I was hungry
when I saw food set before me and asked whose it was.

Anyone who hopes for bananas in wartime runs the risk of
learning the following: that there are no bananas to be had; that
there were never any bananas to begin with; that all bananas had
ever been was a collective fantasy brought on by the deprivations
of war; that your mother will fail to find any bananas; that you will
have to compete with your sisters for the bananas; that your father
will exchange the banana for the experience of watching him eat
the banana, with or without cream and sugar; that your father will
model substitutionary atonement and bear himself your hunger in
his body, Christus Victor, paternal satisfaction, and eat the bananas
in front of you. For such reasons and more a child might not ask
for bread at all but instead say, *I'm not hungry, I ate before I got here.*

Jacob and the Angel Wrasslin' Till Noon at Least

Version One

Jacob arose that night and took his two wives, his two female servants, and his eleven sons, and crossed over the ford of Jabbok. He took them, sent them over the brook, and sent over what he had. Then Jacob was left alone; and a man wrestled with him until the breaking of day. Now when the man saw that he did not prevail against him, he touched the socket of his hip; and the socket of Jacob's hip was out of joint as he wrestled with him. And he said, "Let me go, for the day breaks."

But Jacob said, "I will not let you go unless you bless me!"

So the man said to him, "What is your name?"

He said, "Jacob."

And the man said, "Your name shall no longer be called Jacob, but Israel; for you have struggled with God and with men, and have prevailed."

Then Jacob asked, saying, "Tell me your name, I pray."

And he said, "Why is it that you ask about my name?" And he blessed him there.

So Jacob called the name of the place Peniel: "For I have seen God face to face, and my life is preserved." Just as he crossed over Peniel the sun rose on him, and he limped on his hip.

Version Two

Jacob said, "You guys go on ahead, I'll catch up in a second," and pretended to be looking for something until everyone else dropped out of sight. Then all of a sudden he was wrestling.

"I feel like we just skipped something," Jacob said to the man suddenly wrapped around him. But the man said nothing, just kept wrestling.

"Okay," Jacob said. "I guess this is not the talking kind of wrestling?" Still no answer.

Eventually the sun came up, which means there were at least eight or nine hours of solid, speechless wrestling before that, which, *yikes*, and at which point the man said, "Stop hitting yourself."

What else was there for Jacob to answer? "Stop hitting *your*self."

The man considered it. "I'll stop hitting you if you stop hitting yourself."

So Jacob shut up and kept wrestling. I don't know wrestling maneuvers. Let's say his next move was a pile driver.

"*Asshole*," the angel said, sweating.

"You're the asshole," Jacob answered.

"Let me go," the angel said, "for the day breaks."

"Oh, now we're talking?" Jacob said (still wrestling. Picture a lot of dynamic action, the kind that lends itself well to short, snappy dialogue). "All night long it's sudden and unprompted wordless wrestling with you, but once it starts affecting your schedule, then it's all, 'Oh, hath the day risen, time to be moving along, if it suits

you.' Well, it isn't convenient, and it don't suit me, so prepare yourself to wrassle till noon at least, guy."

And the angel took that moment to press a finger lightly across
the socket of Jacob's hip, which was just entirely too much, and
Jacob lost it.

"Fuck," he said. "Fuck *fuck*, I need a minute." He stepped back,
collapsed into a sort of half crouch, and wrapped his arms around
his knees.

"I'm sorry," the angel said after a pause.

"I didn't say fuck you," Jacob said. "I was just saying fuck. I
wasn't expecting that."

"I wasn't expecting it, either."

"Not really the same thing," Jacob said without looking up, "given
that it wasn't your hip."

The angel sat down next to him. (But not too close.) "Would
you like a blessing?"

"Obviously I would like a blessing," Jacob said. "I'd also appreciate an explanation and an apology, but I'll take a blessing, too."

"Okay. What's your name?"

"Fuck you. What's your name?" Then: "Sorry. That was reflexive."

"It's fine," the angel said, "but I still can't answer it."

"Jacob, J-A-C-O-B."

"Not anymore it's not," the angel said, and then for the next
part imagine that Jacob said, *The shit are you talking about, it's not?*
at the same time the angel said, this time in a real serious voice,
because by this time he'd caught his breath from all the wrestling,
"Now you are Israel, for you have struggled with God and with
men and prevailed."

"The shit are you talking about, it's not?" Israel said again after
a moment's pause. "Asshole. *Asshole!* You show up, mid-night, mid-
wrestle, without a word of explanation or set of rules to agree on,

and then you—*do* that—and then you promise to bless me and instead pull a bush-league stunt like taking my name out of my mouth."

"I don't know," the angel said. "Do you mean when I touched you on the hip socket? I've never done that before. I didn't know how else to get you to stop wrestling. Does it hurt?"

"We just wrestled for nine hours. Everything hurts." Israel shifted in his seat. "I should say, everything *but* that hurts. You, you show up, and you fight me, and then you touch me, and now I have a different name I'm going to have to explain to everyone."

"All of those are excellent points," the angel said. "I rather wish I had not touched you on the hip socket, either, for my own reasons."

Then Israel asked, saying, "Tell me your name, I pray."

And he said, "Why is it that you ask about my name?"

"You're not the only one who can name things," Israel said.

"I never said I was the only one who can name things," the angel said. "But I'm not authorized to answer that particular question. *Do* you want to name something?"

"Yeah, I want to fucking name something," Israel said. "Obviously I want to do that."

"You can name this," the angel said, gesturing toward the rock they'd spent the night wrestling on top of.

"You changed my name for the rest of my life and I get to name a rock?"

And the angel just spread out his hands in response.

"Fuck this," Israel said, hauling himself up awkwardly on his left leg. "Fuck this, fuck you, fuck this rock—Peniel, by the way, short for 'God has once again failed to kill me;' fuck Peniel, fuck daybreak, fuck blessings." Then: "Touch it again."

The angel hesitated. "I'm not authorized to do that."

"I'm not asking you to do it professionally. I'm asking *you*. I want you to do it again; I want to test a theory, and I'm asking you to do me one-half of a small favor after a series of real unnecessary dick moves."

I don't happen to know what the angel did next, whether he touched it again or he didn't. Either way, Israel started walking across Peniel shortly thereafter, sun shining on his forehead, heading directly toward Jabbok, trying to think of an explanation for everyone.

CHAPTER 9

Mary and Martha and Jesus and the Dishes

Now it happened as they went that Jesus entered a certain village; and a certain woman named Martha welcomed Him. And she had a sister called Mary, who also sat at Jesus' feet and heard His word. But Martha was distracted with much serving, and she approached Him and said, "Lord, do You not care that my sister has left me to serve alone? Therefore tell her to help me."

And Jesus answered and said to her, "Martha, Martha, you are worried and troubled about many things. But one thing is needed, and Mary has chosen that good part, which will not be taken away from her."

—Luke 10:38–42

Now it happened that the dishwasher was broken, and that I tried starting it but it kept making that thwumpa-thwumpa *sound instead of turning over, so I just left the dishes in the sink. I don't know if you needed them for dinner. I would have washed them myself, but they never seem to get as clean as when you do them—probably because I do a purposefully half-hearted job of scrubbing in order to get you to do it without asking me for help.*

Also, I've noticed that the house is out of toilet paper, but instead of buying more I plan on tearing little strips of paper towels and layering them carefully over the old toilet paper roll (which I will not throw away). I will do this indefinitely until you buy more toilet paper.

And I hit START on the load of clothes that were sitting in the dryer, which were already finished drying, but which I did not wish to fold; this way when you get home it will sound like they have just finished drying when it buzzes, and you will be the one to fold them.

I have intentionally lowered my standard of living so that when you say things like "This place is a mess," rather than acknowledge the implicit request for acknowledgment or respect or help I can simply grunt, neither agreeing nor disagreeing, and not having to do anything, knowing that eventually you will do all the work necessary to make yourself happy.

Now, *either* one imagines Martha in the middle of serving when she asks this question, possibly elbow-deep in a sinkful of dishes, trying to wipe a flyaway strand of hair off her forehead with a sweaty elbow, in which case being informed that she's troubled "about many things" is both rude and self-evident. One might rather imagine the question coming up throughout the course of an ordinary day, a request to compare and rank their respective vocations without the immediate emergency of having nothing to eat lunch with. But one thing is certain: it is illegal, according to God, for women to wash dishes. Someone else is going to have to do it.

When I was twenty-five I flew to London to spend a week with a man who used to be in love with me but wasn't anymore. Every day he left for work and I would wash all the dishes that were left in the sink from the night before; then I would walk around the neighborhood and weep until it was time for him to come home, where I would pretend to have spent an exciting day *not* crying and wait for him to notice I had washed and put away all the dishes. He did not bother about the dishes, and then I would wait for him to fall asleep and crawl out into his tiny bathroom and cry in the shower. I did this for six days in a row, and grew so frantic by the end that I came up with excuses to furnish him with extra dishes to use, making cup after cup of coffee or suggesting we make pasta so eventually he'd be forced to consider how there could possibly be another mug or colander available, since for all he knew he hadn't done the dishes in a week. It's an embarrassing story for a number of reasons, not least because I fear the moral of the story could be misrepresented as *If you can't get your lousy boyfriend to pick up after himself, become your own lousy boyfriend instead*, or worse, that my failure to demand my rights as a woman directly resulted in my opting for Door Number Two and transitioning as a means of avoiding difficult conversations about housework. What remains true about the story is that I wanted this man, like all men, to immediately and intuitively recognize something in me they consistently failed to notice, and, when that failed, I attempted to make myself so helpful and unobtrusive I would become necessary to their comfort if not to their happiness, and when that failed I ran away to face my own dishes at home.

A few years later, when I went from passively ignoring to actively resisting the question of transition, I stopped cleaning up after myself entirely. I lived alone at the time, so there was no question of inconveniencing or blaming someone else. The idea of tending to anything that belonged to me—my home, my clothes, my appearance—was unbearable, because everything at that time depended on my not having a body. Washing the dishes meant acknowledging that I had hands to wash them with, a stomach to fill, a hunger to address, a body to nourish. I was worried and troubled about many things, although only one thing was needed. I preferred to worry about many things. The work of not doing the dishes is much more complicated and exhausting than doing the dishes, and involves sticking to a strict schedule:

Step One: Begin to avoid the kitchen. If the kitchen cannot be avoided, if it must be passed through in order to reach more desirable environs, like the out-of-doors, avert your eyes from the sink and neighboring counters. The kitchen is now formally Unlovely; do not treat it with affection.

Step Two: Designate a particular coffee mug as the Mug. The Mug is part of your body now and may be reused for any and all beverages, whether coffee or not-yet-flat, this-is-still-good Red Bull, nicotine gum wrappers still sparking with aluminum and chemicals, soups (including ice cream). You might rinse the cup out every now and again, but do not feel the need to formally wash it any more than you would scrub your mouth out with soap and water in between meals; the Mug is as much an extension of your body as your hand or your face.

Step Three: The sink is a place for stacking things and leaving, nothing more.

Step Four: If the sink *must* be addressed, employ a Tetris-style restacking strategy, drizzle everything with watered-down dish soap, turn the faucet on for a few seconds, and announce that you're "leaving these to soak." This qualifies as a chore, and no one can accuse you of task-shying.

Step Five: "It's growing and growing, there's more of it every day, if it's possible to speak of more *nothing*. All the others fled in time . . . but we didn't want to leave our home. The Nothing [of *Neverending Story* fame] caught us in our sleep and this is what it did to us."

"Is it very painful?" Atreyu asked.

"No," said the second bark troll, the one with the hole in his chest. "You don't feel a thing. There's just something missing. And once it gets hold of you, something more is missing every day. Soon there won't be anything left of us."

Step Six: When the stacking balance fails you and topples over, leave the house and take your dinner in a dark corner of a dark restaurant. Place a paper towel on top of the soapy, crumb-filled mess that has oversloshed the kitchen counter, as a sign of penance.

Step Seven: If you have a dishwasher, open it for a few hours—"to let the air in"—and close it sometime after sunset. That's enough for one day.

Step Eight: "And he went a little farther, and fell on his face, and prayed, saying, O my Father, if it be possible, let this cup pass from me: nevertheless not as I will, but as thou wilt" (Matt. 26:39).

Step Nine: Throw something you need very much in the garbage.

Step Ten: "Is it very painful?" Atreyu asked. "Is it very painful?" Is it? Is it very painful? Is it painful? Is it very? Is it very painful? Is it very painful?

And so on, until your life cracks open and God addresses you by your name twice to make sure that he's gotten your attention. The question then becomes what it is, exactly, that Mary has chosen. Martha seems to think *the work*, whatever the work is, has fallen exclusively to her. Jesus declines to call what Mary does either *work* or *not work*, describing it instead as "what is needed," sometimes "what is better," sometimes "what is good." Every so often it is written "what is best." The question that kept me from my own dishes was the question of whether transition was *necessary* or merely *good*, namely whether I could get away with avoiding it. I wanted to know my other options. I wanted to see a different menu. I wanted a guarantee that my only alternative to transition was ruin, because to take that risk on any other terms was totally unacceptable to me; I wanted to be informed that I either *had to* or *could not* do it, assigned a formal vocation rather than encouraged to discern one. What can Martha do, at the end of that conversation? If she has been chastened, it was lovingly done; but she has received very little guidance about the nature of her own work. Is Mary's part the best for her, too? Should she join her sister in formal discipleship? Should she compare the two of them together more often, or less? She knows more about Mary, certainly, but not if her own work is *good* or *good enough* or *good-for-Martha* or something else. What I wanted at the outset of transition was the opportunity to fold back the page at this particular turning point and live forward in two directions at once, in one version of my life where I transitioned and in one where I didn't, then revisit after about fifteen solid years in each reality and make an informed assessment of which life proved the better. I had no interest in keeping my eyes only on my own work. I wanted my work, and everyone else's, and for someone else to come and help me with mine in the bargain. I wanted a guaranteed outcome before moving forward. I wanted what was best, and I wanted to know what was best in advance, with frequent updates to follow just in case the good or the better suddenly moved into the lead.

Brother Lawrence offers a third possible perspective on the problem of dishes and vocation (which may or may not have been Martha's problem after all):

> He does not ask much of us, merely a thought of Him from time to time, a little act of adoration, sometimes to ask for His grace, sometimes to offer Him your sufferings, at other times to thank Him for the graces, past and present, He has bestowed on you, in the midst of your troubles to take solace in Him as often as you can. Lift up your heart to Him during your meals and in company; the least little remembrance will always be the most pleasing to Him. One need not cry out very loudly; He is nearer to us than we think . . . We can do little things for God; I turn the cake that is frying on the pan for love of Him, and that done, if there is nothing else to call me, I prostrate myself in worship before Him, who has given me grace to work; afterwards I rise happier than a king. It is enough for me to pick up but a straw from the ground for the love of God.

Brother Lawrence, of course, never had my or Martha's problem with the dishes, having neatly sidestepped a number of psychosexual dish-adjacent issues by only doing the washing-up in a monastery. But there is a neatness to it, particularly for a spiritually anxious transsexual: picture a sacred presence, dress it up as a boy if you like, who not only *notices* every time you bake a cake or unload the dishwasher but delights in it, revels in it, considers it a pure and lovely offering every time you do it. *This is my son, in whom I am well pleased; I see you have done the dishes again.* Trans people sometimes talk about gender euphoria, that expansive sense of purpose and delight that can accompany certain moments in transition; I found myself anxiously scanning my own brain in the first few hours after starting testosterone ("I'm just *trying* it," I told my friends. "I'm not *on* it, exactly, just *trying*, there's a difference"): *Am I euphoric yet? How about now? Is this euphoria? How will I know, if transition has been founded in large part by the realization that I often can't trust my own sense of self, because I used to think I was a cis woman and only belatedly realized I might have been in error?* There was nothing to do for it but continue to go about my life, running the experiment and walking the dog and answering emails and boiling water for tea and putting away dishes as needed, all while paying careful attention. And when the euphoria came—and went, and came back, and settled into something a little more than predictable and a little less than jarring—it was enough to pick up a straw, or put away a dish, all for the love of it.

Columbo in Six Positions

After a little more than two years on testosterone, my voice keeps trembling as well as thumping down the octave scale every couple of weeks. With every deepening I lose another of what I once considered my reliable impressions. My impressions used to be delivered almost exclusively to myself in the car or in the shower, but I miss them just the same. They were especially useful when I wanted to rehearse arguments I planned on having and needed to assign a certain type of personality to my imaginary interlocutors. I recently discovered that my Miranda from *Sex and the City* is completely gone, my Joan Didion is a mess, my Kate Hepburn sounds mannered and forced—not in the way that Kate sounded mannered and forced, but in a way that makes my ears question the sex of my throat. I love very much the baffling little burr of my new vocal cords, but I have no idea where all this is going.

They were not many, my impressions, and they were never stellar, but they took me a lifetime to assemble and only about six months to torpedo, so I've been trying to figure out what's going to take their place. I have been able, with careful study, to develop a rudimentary, preverbal Columbo, the first man I ever loved. I cannot yet trust myself to mimic the voice, as I keep going wide and skidding headfirst into "central casting New York City beat officer in a midcentury musical," so this is all pantomime, but I would nevertheless like to invite you to share in my process. Someday soon I will be ready to speak.

COLUMBO—FIRST POSITION

This will be the attitude from which all more complex Columbos develop. Wherever you are standing, take a step back, while bobbing your head apologetically downward. Allow belligerent deference to bend your spine. Retract the two top vertebrae. Tilt your head to whatever side feels more unnatural. Draw down your features until you feel like you're making a sort of "Robert De Niro doesn't like this idea that's being presented to him" expression. Pinch the left side of your mouth up, your left eye and eyebrow down into a wink. Place both hands with palms facing outward just in front of your face, keeping the thumbs pointed at each other and letting the rest of your fingers droop slightly. This is the Columbo of preparation, of anticipation, of eternal readiness. Breathe. Not deeply, nor restfully, but like a basset hound bent on justice, or half an accordion.

COLUMBO—SECOND POSITION

While maintaining first position, thrust your left hand forward as far as it can go while keeping it at eye level, dropping your three left fingers so that your pointer finger extends directly upward to God and your thumb acts as a counterweight. Pull your right hand slightly closer to your face. Pulse your left hand back and forth, as if it were asking a question. Furrow your eyebrows further, if they're not already maximally furrowed. The truth is a very heavy jewel, and it hovers somewhere in the middle of your face; all of your features are inexorably drawn toward it.

COLUMBO—THIRD POSITION

Pass your right hand over your face, gently pressing your first and third fingers against your forehead, brushing your thumb over your right cheek, and letting the palm lightly graze the tip of your nose. Retract your left arm toward your body until your elbow is at a right angle. Keep the right hand light; you are not burying your face in your hands in anguish, but brushing off insincerity.

COLUMBO—FOURTH POSITION

Bring the left hand up to the side of your face, rubbing your first two fingers against the temple. Leave the right hand as it is. Scrunch both eyes closed, then open them wide. Yawn without parting your lips. Columbo never opens his mouth before the time is right.

COLUMBO—FIFTH POSITION

I know something needs to go here. I just don't know what yet. Guess it's a mystery.

COLUMBO—SIXTH POSITION

Draw both hands up and over the head, scrunching whatever hair you have between the ear and the crown between your fingers. Lean back from the shoulders, while simultaneously maintaining an overall attitude of ducking, as if before a suspicious God. Continue furrowing the left side of your face, while letting the right side go slack and relaxed (or slack and weary, as you prefer). An answer is coming.

On Wednesdays We
Mean Girls Wore Pink

R

I get hit by the same bus every day. At least I think I do. I don't always know the difference between what I know and what I think. But I do know that it hurts, every time. And the day is always divided into before I get hit by the bus, and after I get hit by the bus, but it hurts on both sides. Sometimes I'm in the hospital, sometimes I'm at home, resting. Everyone calls it resting. I don't know what they mean by that. I don't know that resting is the best response to being hit by a bus. But I do it anyhow. Sometimes I'm back at school, and I'm in the middle of a conversation that I didn't even know I was having, and I'll think, *I think I was just hit by a bus*, but no one around me is *acting* like I just got hit by a bus, so I act like I wasn't hit by a bus, either.

Sometimes it's hard to distinguish between what I know and what there is to know. I'll know—I'll *think* I know—something, like "Everyone in Africa can read Swedish." But I'm not sure if I know that. So I try to run tests in my own head before I say something. I'll ask, *Where in Africa do I think people can read Swedish?* And then I'll think: *I don't know.* And then I'll ask, *Can I name a*

*specific country in Africa where people read Swedish? And then I'll ask,
Can I name a specific country in Africa at all? Do I know where Sweden
is?* And I can't, and so I think, *I probably don't know that after all.* So
I don't say anything.

C

I heard she got hit by a bus. But hearing someone got hit by a bus,
and actually getting hit by a bus, those are two different things.

Once, I was on a stage and I split something very important into
pieces. I gave the pieces to everyone I could reach. I think that's sort
of what happened to her.

It wasn't a party, exactly, and I don't remember what I was onstage
for. But someone handed me something beautiful, and I cracked it
open. I think afterward people applauded. I don't remember why.

Now I have a boyfriend who lives very far away. I don't know
when I'm going to see him again. I don't remember if he's trapped,
or missing. But I know he's somewhere very far away, and I know
that sometimes I feel like I'm just floating. If I think about what's
happening around me very carefully, I can sometimes get a sense
of whether he's here, if he has his arm around me or if it's someone
else, or if anyone has their arm around me at all. I don't know what
he does with his arms when he's not here, or how he gets here at all,
or what happens when he goes away. I don't think he's here right
now. But I'm not sure. I know it's never her arm around me. I would
remember that. I think I would remember that. One of us would
remember. There is a limit that exists there.

But the bus has never hit me. It comes close, sometimes, but it's
never happened to me. There is no limit there.

D

My curfew is 1:00 a.m. I don't have anything else to say about
this. About what's happening to everyone. What's been happen-

ing to everyone. I'm not getting out of the car, and I'm going home.

J

I'm not going to apologize. So it doesn't matter, whether I wish I could apologize, or whether I thought I was wrong, or whether—it doesn't matter, because I'm not going to apologize, because nobody else seemed to think that I should. So I don't get to. Everyone else gets to, and I don't.

M

Michigan isn't in Africa. I don't know why I have to keep telling people that. Well. I know why. But I wish they would remember that I've said it before.

Maybe I'll stop telling people I'm from Michigan. Maybe then something different will happen.

Maybe tomorrow I will ask everyone, "Are you from Michigan?" again and again until someone admits the truth.

D

For the record, I don't like it when she says it, either. But you pick your battles.

J

Did he say he didn't like it when I say it, either? He did, didn't he? But he didn't say that he doesn't like it to me. So what am I supposed to do with that?

R

I've never eaten cheese fries. I've never actually gone shopping, if I'm honest. I just drive around for hours until eventually I'm the only one left in the car. Then I go—home, I think? I go somewhere. When I go home, the phone is ringing, and there's a woman's voice on the other end of the line. She always wants something from me, but I can never make out what she's saying. She never hangs up, so neither do I, and we fall asleep to the sound of each other's questions.

D

She could stop saying it.

R

I know that there is only one pair of pants that fit me right now. But I don't know where they are. And I'm not going to ask anyone. It's not that I don't trust them. It's that I don't know if trust is a reasonable expectation to have of another person.

J

I was never talking about you, when I said that. When I said—that thing I always said. The thing you don't like me to say.

D

I know that. Do you think I didn't know that?

J

Then why—okay. Okay. I don't think I knew that you knew. And I didn't know that I knew. And—you should know—you know that I'm not going to apologize about it. I can't. But I won't say it again.

D

I *function*.

J

I know you do.

D

I function like an *ecosystem* functions. Like a *galaxy* functions. I *function.*

J

Maybe *you* should have joined the Mathletes.

D

Is that a *joke*?

J

Yes.

D

It's a good joke. You should tell that kind of joke more often.

J

Look—
    Okay. Maybe I should.

D

And I'm on the Mathletes.

J

You are?

D

I'm an alternate. Three years running.

J

You know I can't say it.

D

You could say it. It's not as hard as you think it is.

But you don't have to say it.

G

I don't speak Vietnamese. And—obviously—they know I don't speak it, but they never do anything about it, and there's always a seat there for me, so I keep coming back, and I think, *God, just please don't let me say anything today*, but then I can feel it coming over me all in a rush, and I hear myself start to speak whatever it is that I'm saying, and I'm horrified, but I can't stop. I wish someone would stop me. I wish I would stop me.

K

Ever since she got hit by that bus, I can't stop coughing. "I'm sick," I say, and people nod their heads like they're agreeing with me, but then nobody does anything, or says anything in response. So I don't think I know what agreeing is. I thought I did, but it can't be this. It can't be nodding your head and not doing anything. Maybe I'm not sick at all. Maybe I'm sicker than anyone has ever been, and that's why nobody's doing anything.

A

There was a week—I think it was a week—when I knew, I absolutely *knew* that everyone around me wanted me to go to the projection room above the auditorium. Everyone wanted me to go to the same place, at the same time, and for the same reason, but no one *asked* me to do it. They kept trying to—I would see people I knew, but they weren't the people I knew. They were in disguise. I know how that sounds, but they were. They were all a part of it. And I didn't know why. I just know that I hated it.

R

I don't know why we still have the bus. The day is going to be over soon, and the bus is going to come, and nobody is going to do anything about it.

K

Everyone gets pregnant and dies. He was right about that much. That's how I start the morning announcements now. That's all I say. They don't let me on the air anymore, but I keep saying it.

C

The bus is going to split her wide open. Into pieces. But all I can do is solve the problem that's right in front of me. And she's not in front of me right now.

R

Everyone is going to let it happen again. I'm going to let it happen again. And when she calls tonight, I know I'm not going to answer any of her questions.

C

There is a limit to certain things. There is a limit to me.

R

Sweden is a country. I know that. I know that I know that. Africa not a country. Africa is a continent with fifty-four countries, none of which is Sweden. I know that. I know that I know that. I looked it up in the library today. I've never eaten cheese fries, and I've never gone shopping, and I never put my arm around her. I'm never going to. I don't know that. I only think that. Maybe I will put my arm around her tomorrow, or maybe she will put her arm around me.

When the bell rings, I will get up and I will go outside, even if I don't want to, and the bus will come or not come, and then something else will happen. Something else is always happening.

C

Whenever someone has put something beautiful in front of me, I have always tried to solve it. I don't know if that's something I should apologize for or not.

J

I'm not going to say it.

D

She thinks that she can't say it until someone makes her say it, but that's not how anything works.

CHAPTER 10

The Golden Girls and the Mountains in the Sea

Midway this way of life we're bound upon,
I woke to find myself in a dark wood,
Where the right road was wholly lost and gone.

Ay me! How hard to speak of it that rude
And rough and stubborn forest! The mere breath
Of memory stirs the old fear in the blood.
> —Dante Alighieri, *The Divine Comedy: Inferno*,
> translated by Dorothy L. Sayers

I first came to experience transition as a series of structural collapses. Before I had any sense of what I wanted, of what I believed myself to be or need, I experienced a falling-away, a loss of social and physical fluency, a sense of foundationlessness. It is tempting, now, from the relative safety and security of my current position, to absorb that interval into the new narrative of a life that makes sense to me: my old understanding and self-conceptions had to first give way in order for something realer, truer, braver, more radical, more modern, more exciting, more zeitgeisty to take charge, to wrap up various dramatic arcs of my life like a season of television. But I find myself resistant to declaring, *That* was false and *this* is real; *here* I did not know myself and *there* I did; *this* was something not-me and *that* was my true self. This fondness for disavowing old mission statements and replacing them with new ones was, in fact, the most characteristic habit of my drinking days, where every morning brought with it a fresh announcement, a new resolve, a declaration of profound and immediate change, even if the declaration was only broadcast inside my own head and crowded out by more pressing matters by the time I reached the front door. Now *I know what I need to do to get out of this fix. Now I truly know myself, and in knowing myself I can master myself, and by mastering myself I can start building a brand-new future this instant.* Getting sober had less to do with finding a better way to more effectively stick to a new resolve and more to do with permitting collapse and abandoning resistance. I found it both discouraging and distressingly on the nose that transitioning seemed to mirror sobriety in that respect. It *sounds* like an evasion, or at best a euphemistic bromide: "Just stop trying and everything will work itself out somehow!" There are times when I look back over my life and see roots of a potential transition long before I began to consider the possibility. Not ironclad evidence, not portents and prophecies, but something that might have been tended and watered into growth, had I recognized them as being anything capable of growing.

By the time I reached my thirties, I believed the main narrative cycle of my adult life had been resolved. Not *finished*, of course, but having achieved the kind of balance I assumed was a natural result of addressing the main hindrances to my personal growth, I envisioned a future that simply played out gratifying, interchangeable variations on the major themes of the present: A financially self-sufficient woman, who ran her own business and managed her own career, living independently and liking it, contentedly childless with perhaps the occasional wistful fantasy of what might have been, extolling the pleasures of eating alone and wearing caftans, entirely and cheerfully divorced from the world of men. A one-woman *Golden Girls* act (never mind that the *Golden Girls* ends with Dorothy getting married and leaving the rest of the girls behind to run a hotel in Miami). The story of my life, then, was for years that I was a woman because it did not occur to me that I might have other options, if I cared to investigate them. And there were so many wonderful things about being a woman! If I experienced moments of dismay, or disappointment, or discontentedness, that was easy enough to account for; life is often made difficult for women, so those moments were in themselves further evidence for my cis womanhood. Then came the question, the sudden uncertainty, the loss of faith in my future, the giving-way of self-satisfaction to panic. I imagined the solution to my problem to look something like this:

SELF: "Excuse me, my womanness is broken and I'd like to speak to the manager of . . . girls, I suppose, so that someone can repair it or exchange it for another womanhood of comparable value."

MANAGER: "Ah, welcome to Being-a-Woman. Yes, I see your problem right here. The good news is that there are *many* ways to be a woman. Here are a few options we have available in your size—if you'd care to step in the back and, ah, try them on? It's a poorly lit fitting room and you'll feel terrible wearing them. That's how you'll know it's working!"

SELF: "Thanks very much. I'll take the gray with the blue trimming. May I have a receipt in case I need to make another exchange later on?"

MANAGER: "But of course. *Bonne journée, madame.*"

Followed, of course, by a graceful exit and a renewed zest for living.

The story of my drinking had been much the same. If I experienced moments of panic, or terror, or loss, or mental degradation, or bewilderment, or lost time, or found myself in places I did not wish to be, that was easy enough to account for, too; there was something broken with my drinking and I needed a better drinking strategy, of which there were thousands, if not tens of thousands. So many ways to be a drunk, so many ways to be a woman; it was simply a matter of trying another set of combinations and waiting for them to take effect. I continued to drink long after drinking had stopped working, by which I mean it no longer reliably produced the same familiar cycle of crisis-panic-abandonment-release-crisis that enabled me to feel like my life contained useful forward momentum. Entering into sobriety necessarily involved resigning from the unpaid, unpleasant job of crisis management and developing a new relationship to momentum entirely—not attempting to manufacture it, but attempting to move along with it, and even sometimes attempting to rest in its absence. It required a great deal less work than drinking had. The mental and physical energy required to formulate a brand-new drinking strategy; create a plan for off-loading shame and avoiding disaster; pilot a worn-out body into work reliably enough to keep a job; and steel my nerves for the hours between the old hangover and the next day's drunkenness was immense. Every day began in fevered preparation for the turnaround that was always just about to begin, in the certainty that *today* I had solved the riddle of how to drink as I needed to without giving anyone else cause for concern or finding myself in the hospital—as if I had just discovered I was about to come into a great inheritance, and needed to prepare my house and my body and my social life and my bank account for the new and glorious work of stewarding that inheritance.

The delusion that this work was real or meaningful or profitable to me in any way was persistent, impenetrable, and deadly. Progress, at least in terms of sobriety, looked at first like regression, like loss: loss of certainty, of direction, of habit, of routine, of activity, of the ability to envision a recognizable future, of the sense of momentum. But what I experienced first as loss I would go on to experience as necessary, invigorating, useful, even pleasant. Even, on occasion, as a relief.

Transition was much the same way. After a year of trying very hard every day not to transition, trying to isolate, control, and obliterate the desire to pursue it, giving up the idea that I could manage myself out of my own body came as such a relief. "Come to Me, all you who labor and are heavy laden, and I will give you rest. Take My yoke upon you and learn from Me, for I am gentle and lowly in heart, and you will find rest for your souls. For My yoke is easy and My burden is light" (Matthew 11:28–30). But I had to desire rest for my soul more than I desired to cling to cis-ness, and I fought that exchange every step of the way. It was too late, I was both too young and too old, I should have said something sooner, it would not work for me the way it worked for other people, I would lose my family, I would be reneging on the promise my body had made to others, I would humiliate myself, I *needed* the heavy yoke, deserved it, owed it to the people in my life to go on carrying it; I did not believe an easy yoke existed for me.

One of the most common admonitions in the Bible is "fear not." Sometimes it is offered as advice, sometimes as reassurance, sometimes as command. Sometimes death and disaster follow regardless, as in Genesis 35, where a midwife counsels Rachel not to despair as she delivers her son before dying. So "fear not" is not the same as a promise that all will be well, that life will go on. Rachel, dying, names her son Ben-Oni; Genesis tells us that her husband Jacob goes on to rename him Benjamin, though it does not say why; nor does it say whether Rachel died in a condition of fearlessness or despair. But we who read the story are told the name she chose, even if no one ever called her son by that name except herself.

One might understandably grow a little frustrated, encountering the same reminder to *be not afraid* again and again, especially if one interprets it as an instruction missing a few key details about how, exactly, not to fear. It is the same frustration shared by the alcoholic who wants to just *stop drinking*, the transition-shy who want to just *stop thinking about it*. It reads better, I think, if one considers *fear not* to be a descriptive rather than a prescriptive remark, as informative rather than exhortative. The feeling of safety and the condition of safety are not the same; it is both the nature and the purview of God to exchange the former for the latter. So it is that the forty-sixth Psalm reads,

> God is our refuge and strength,
> a very present help in trouble.
> Therefore we will not fear,
> Even though the earth be removed,
> And though the mountains be carried into the midst of the sea;
> Though its waters roar and be troubled,
> Though the mountains shake with its swelling. *Selah*

This is no mere anxious fancy—there is reason enough here to be afraid. Destruction and death are at hand, mountains develop rootlessness and the foundational security of the earth itself is at risk. More distressing than even the prospect of the earth's wholesale removal is the description of God's career:

> Come, behold the works of the Lord,
> Who has made desolations in the earth.
> He makes wars cease to the end of the earth;

He breaks the bow and cuts the spear in two;
He burns the chariot in the fire.

Be still, and know that I am God;
I will be exalted among the nations,
I will be exalted in the earth!

The invitation to come and look on desolation, to prepare for
God's inevitable and terrifying exaltation, the reminder that wars
can be finished—not *ended*, merely *finished*—at the unknowable
whim of the divine is hardly reassuring in the face of mortal fear.
The source of safety, then, cannot come from a certainty that dan-
gers will pass and one will be permitted to resume the previous
course of one's life. It is a portrait of God that is bewildering, con-
clusive, irresistible not in the manner of being delightedly drawn in
but in the manner of being devastated, unaccountable. The Psalm-
ist suggests that true safety, then, cannot be found in what seems
secure, cannot be found in reliability or predictability or contented-
ness, that desolation will come and must be met rather than fore-
stalled or foreclosed upon, that safety itself lies upon the other side
of the fire and the broken chariot and the collapse of the mountains
into the sea. One might be forgiven for seeing such an account and
deciding against the idea of safety altogether.

The first time I actively sought out the company of trans people
came after I gave up on the idea that I was going to solve the problem of wanting things by sitting alone in my room trying as hard as I
could not to want anything. It was a terrible, dizzying day; I wanted
more than anything for solitary despair and self-recrimination to
provide me with the tools to build a bright and livable future, never
mind that solitary despair had never produced anything for me
but additional solitary despair. I snuck into a local trans support
group well after the meeting had started in an act of complete sur-

render, having given up yet again on the fantasy of the successful operation of crisis management. Progress looked, once again, like regression: I had failed to cope, failed to maintain a secure and sufficient cisgender sense of self, failed to force peace upon myself. I was emotional, embarrassing; bewitched, bothered, and bewildered. Worse still, my greatest fears were realized when I entered the room: I felt comforted in the presence of other trans people. It was not that I felt immediate kinship and recognition with everyone in the room—many of us had relatively little in common, some of them I liked and some I did not—but the effect was nonetheless immediate and came in the manner of a reprieve after a long day's thankless work. I experienced relief when I had not come seeking relief but resolution and a promise that the mountains would return to their original position at my command. The forty-sixth Psalm and the Friday night meeting of trans Californians served as a necessary reminder that the mountains do not move under my imperative, and that safety cannot ever be reached in trying harder to make sure my orders are obeyed by things that fall outside of my personal power.

Jesus in the Gospels tells a number of stories about the kingdom of heaven, sometimes also the kingdom of God; whether the two are interchangeable or merely closely linked is a matter of some debate. He does not spend a great deal of time explaining what the kingdom of heaven *is*, but in alerting others to its presence. *It is like a seed, it is like a net, it is like a pearl of great price hidden in a field, it is like yeast, it is like a merchant who comes across a pearl of great price hidden in a field, it is like a king preparing a wedding banquet and his uncooperative guests; it is near at hand, it is more than just near at hand but currently present, it is an internal condition, it is an external system of justice, it is expansive, it is restrictive, it is the enemy of wealth and tightfistedness, it is a gift that God takes great pleasure in giving, it is the engine that metes out not just justice but retribution and more than retribution, terror, it is mysterious and far-off, it is like children and for children, it is for the childlike, it is seen and unseen, capable of sudden and rapid growth, bursting through and out and up, continually emerging and becoming more of itself, more real by the second and already real, all-welcoming and difficult to enter.* The Parable of the Sower reads:

> "Listen! Behold, a sower went out to sow. And it happened, as he sowed, that some seed fell by the wayside; and the birds of the air came and devoured it. Some fell on stony ground, where it did not have much earth; and immediately it sprang up because it had no depth of earth. But when the sun was up it was scorched, and because it had no root it withered away. And some seed fell among thorns; and the thorns grew up and choked it, and it yielded no crop. But other seed fell on good ground and yielded a crop that sprang up, increased and produced: some thirtyfold, some sixty, and some a hundred."
>
> And He said to them, "He who has ears to hear, let him hear!"
>
> —Mark 4:3–9

This served as a guidepost to me throughout various moments of heartsickness and fear and doubt and hope and joy along my transition, which grew more real by the second and as a result more real retroactively, which was all-welcoming and difficult to enter, which was seen and unseen, capable of sudden and rapid growth, bursting through and out and up, continually emerging and becoming more itself. I often thought, too, of Dorothy Zbornak and her exit from *The Golden Girls*, a show I often watched on repeat in the evenings when sleep became impossible and sometimes in the afternoon when everything else seemed impossible, too. I'd grown up watching Rose and Blanche and Dorothy and Sophia in reruns, but somehow I'd never seen the series finale or had any sense of how the show had ended.

I'd been dimly aware of the existence of *The Golden Palace*, the single-season spinoff that didn't feature Bea Arthur, who played Dorothy, but I hadn't expected that the last episode of *The Golden Girls* would actually show her *leaving*. One afternoon a friend of mine came over to keep my company and we spent a few hours watching episodes from the first two seasons of the show. I had to leave the house to run an errand, and when I came back my friend was watching "One Flew Out of the Cuckoo's Nest, Part I," which I assumed was still part of the early series run. All I knew was that it was a two-parter that featured Leslie Nielsen. I figured, based on the title, that there'd be a strange, farcical spell of some form of institutionalization, like David Duchovny's arc on *Sex and the City*, and I thought that was sort of a strange direction for the show to take in a brief run, but I generally like Leslie Nielsen's work and had a lot of faith in *The Golden Girls'* writing staff, so I went with it.

It was a fantastic arc, maybe the best *Golden Girls* episode I'd seen, even though the plot was absolutely bananas. Dorothy and Nielsen's Lucas pretend to get engaged to cheese off Blanche, only to actually fall in love with each other. Oddly, no one else in the cast ever discovers that their engagement started out as a put-on, so when they get engaged-for-real a second time, all the other girls just sort of shrug and accept it as a quirk. Dorothy's ex-husband, Stanley, drives her to the church and offers her his blessing in the form of a rambling monologue about his hairlessness:

"Do you see this hair? It is the only one on my forehead. The other traitors receded years ago, but this proud and loyal sprout clings desperately. It is unrelenting. It is true. Dorothy, it is this hair I hate more than all the others. It mocks me. Don't you see? I am that hair. And you're my big, crazy, bald skull. I may give you some reason to resent me, but you cannot shake me. I am loyal."

One of the things I'd feared most about starting testosterone therapy was the idea of losing my hair, that I might arrive to manhood late enough that its first fruits would be male-pattern baldness, that I would have made a foolish bargain trading away being a reasonably pretty woman for a single proud and loyal sprout of hair mocking my head. Dorothy's response to this man is, as always, dry, fond, and exasperated, utterly uninterested in humoring male vanity by avoiding the truth: "Stanley, you wore a toupee for twenty-seven years."

And then she marries Leslie Nielsen, and then she moves away. That's the end of the show.

I kept watching in increasing confusion, thinking, *They're going to have to come up with some reason to get rid of him really fast, because I know the next five seasons of* The Golden Girls *don't prominently feature Leslie Nielsen as Dorothy's husband Lucas, who lives next door and is always stopping by for iced tea and cheesecake.* But they don't get rid of him; he marries Dorothy and they move away. I didn't know the end was coming—I didn't even know what I was watching was the end of something. I proceeded to entirely *lose it*, and started sobbing in front of my friend. We had watched the pilot episode only a few hours before. I had thought we had more time. In the very first episode, Blanche almost moves out of their shared home to get married, but her fiancé turns out to be a bigamist and a con artist who gets arrested right before the ceremony. Blanche takes to her bed for three weeks. She finally comes out of her room to talk to the rest of the girls:

BLANCHE: At first I wanted to give up, to die, truly. Only time I ever felt worse was when George died. But then I had the kids with me and I pulled through it. This time, I thought, "This is my last chance, my last hope for happiness." I just thought I'd never feel good again.

SOPHIA: How long is this story? I'm eighty. I have to plan.

BLANCHE: This morning I woke up and I was in the shower, shampooing my hair, and I heard humming. I thought there was someone in there with me. No, it was me. I was humming. And humming means I'm feeling good. And then I realized I was feeling good because of you. You made the difference. You're my family, and you make me happy to be alive.

ROSE: Let's drive to Coconut Grove for lunch.

BLANCHE: Okay!

ROSE: My treat. We have to celebrate.

SOPHIA: What, that she came out of her room?

ROSE: That we're together.

DOROTHY: And that no matter what happens, even if we all get married, we'll stick together.

ROSE: Then we'll need a much bigger house.

DOROTHY: Sure, Rose.

And I kept trying to explain that to a friend, through tears, that I felt betrayed by a long-since-canceled sitcom about a house of retirees. That show, that particular vision of retirement, had *promised* me something, implicitly, or rather through that show and other visions like it I had promised myself something I could now no longer keep. My security had rested in a sort of negotiation with compulsory heterosexuality, such that when all my friends had outlived their husbands, we'd all get to move in together and eat cheesecake and wear comfortable loungewear for our seven extra statistically predetermined years of life. Whatever else might change in life, we could at least count on that. And that even if we got married, even if we married men, we weren't going anywhere in terms of our relationship to one another; the show wasn't called *The Golden Placeholders Until I Meet Leslie Nielsen*. It was a negotiation that existed primarily in my own fantasies, of course, but it was a load-bearing fantasy, and the architecture of my mind suffered from the loss of it.

I'd never hated Leslie Nielsen before—I thought the *Naked Gun* movies were overrated, but I didn't blame him for that—but Lord, did I hate him then. He tugged Dorothy through every door in every scene. You could barely keep him in a shot. He was always disappearing just out of frame. *Let's get a move on, let's get out of here, time's a-wasting.* What are you in such a hurry *for*, Leslie? There's no rush. Sit down in the kitchen with the girls and have some iced tea. I didn't mind that Dorothy got married, but I minded that he took her away from that kitchen table. There was room at the table for him, if he'd just pulled up a chair and sat down.

Later that day I tried looking up *The Golden Palace* to see if it would cheer me up, but then I read the plot summary of its own series finale: "Following the cancellation of the series, Sophia returns to the Shady Pines retirement home, appearing as a cast member in the later seasons of *Empty Nest*. What becomes of Rose, Blanche, and the hotel is left unresolved."

My friend attempted to remind me that it was perhaps not especially useful to assign an old sitcom the job of reassuring me that everything was going to be okay, that transition would not take me out of my place in the world or in the lives of the people who loved me, that intimacy does not require total personal immutability, but I still felt for all the world like Mr. Rochester in *Jane Eyre* upon learning that Mr. Mason has arrived, that all of his plans and hopes for the future have come to nothing, that the full force of his past is coming back to claim him, that his attempts to force Jane into the shape of a wife through the sheer force of his desperation and will must prove ultimately fruitless—

"Jane, I've got a blow; I've got a blow, Jane!"

Later I ended up calming down enough to go back to an earlier episode, one where Rose and Dorothy enter a songwriting competition and write a jingle about Miami. I still knew the blow was coming, but once you're prepared for the hit, you can get into position and wait for the force to pass through you. On the other side of sobriety my life was not given over to a daily battle against the desire to drink; after starting to transition my life was not given over to a daily battle against the desire to be a man. One no longer has to fight battles after giving up; something new can happen then. Once you accept that you're going bald you can start to look for toupees; once the mountains are in the sea you can stop imagining they're going to move at your command; once the blow hits, you are free of the dread of the blow, and you can start to mend from it.

CHAPTER 11

Captain James T. Kirk Is a Beautiful Lesbian, and I'm Not Sure Exactly How to Explain That

A while ago I received a copy of William Shatner's latest auto-biography. My friends have a general sense that I have some sort of one-sided relationship to William Shatner that does not extend to wanting to know anything about his personal life, but that's about as far as we usually get on the subject. I haven't read the book yet. Odds are I won't get around to it.

William Shatner, through no particular fault of his own, has always produced in me such a combination of powerful senti-ments, such a furious mixture of longing and frustration and incoherence, that I can scarcely bear to think directly about him. By most accounts he is an unpleasant man and I think it unlikely that we would have much to say to each other, although that's not exactly why I don't want to know what he's thinking or say-ing or working on these days. I have had to remind friends that I don't want to hear about what fights William Shatner is getting into on Twitter, that I do not want ever to be put into a position where I might have to say hello to him, that for us to ever meet would result in great humiliation for me and moderate confusion for him. I have never sought to consummate any of my desires. I could never stand to be in a room with William Shatner. I would almost certainly burst into tears and quite possibly ask to suck his dick, and I can't imagine he needs that kind of vibrantly upsetting energy in his life. I do not know exactly what I would require from him, and my guess is that he has spent probably enough of his life around people who overreact to his presence. The only thing I really want from him is to be left alone so I can contemplate him properly.

William Shatner guest-starred on two different episodes of *Columbo*, but I shall only require you to see the first, from 1976. Shatner's second appearance, 1994's "Butterflies in Shades of Grey," is necessary only for the compulsive Shatner completist. Better to watch "Fade in to Murder." *Columbo*, like the original run of *Star Trek*, regularly tried to imagine how to solve problems without immediately resorting to violence, and showcased a certain sort of competent, empathetic male peacefulness that makes me cry when I try to explain it to someone who's never watched the show.

I have been trying very hard not to talk to you about *Star Trek*, but I'm afraid I'll have to. No one really wants to hear how someone else got into *Star Trek* any more than they want to hear about your dream last night; those stories all sound the same and never quite tell the truth. I will confine myself to this: I had no real choice when it came to loving *Star Wars*. I saw it for the first time when I was six years old and was not yet grown enough to be able to decide where to bestow my adoration. I loved *Star Wars* helplessly, reflexively; I came to it before the age of accountability, which does not apply only to theological matters but those concerning the heart. For example, I was baptized at twelve, yet when it happened, I did not think of myself as too young for it at the time; it is the same way with *Star Wars*. For better or worse, I am a *Star Wars* person. I neither regret nor wish to change that part of myself, but I cannot take credit or responsibility for it. *Star Trek*, however, was something that belonged to me as soon as I saw it, and William Shatner belonged to me most of all. He was always being framed in gauzy close-ups, which was exactly how I wanted to look at the sort of man who compelled me—that is, handsome men of less-than-average height dressed in stretchy, breathable fabrics, with countless best friends committed to nonviolence, who had slightly feminine hips, who solved puzzles, and maintained erotically charged eye contact with other men and lady science officers: *Yes, just like that, more of this, but don't get any closer. Give me the outlines as sharp as you can, but stop zooming in.*

At any rate, Bill Shatner is more than *Star Trek*—or at least I want to believe that he is more than *Star Trek*, which is why I am trying to put off talking about *Star Trek* for as long as possible. In "Fade in to Murder," Bill plays Ward Fowler, an actor famous for playing the television detective "Lieutenant Lucerne." He is also a murderer. He wears lifts in his shoes and a toupee and is following a joyless studio diet to keep his weight down, and spends the majority of the episode sheepishly acknowledging the truth about his body.

"I'd appreciate a certain amount of discretion in that matter, Lieutenant," he tells Columbo after each confession/discovery. "Public image, you know."

I never know how to refer to previous incarnations of myself in a way that honestly acknowledges the present without sacrificing the past. There is truth, sometimes, in saying that I used to be a woman of sorts, although I don't think I'd much appreciate hearing someone else say this about me. Let us say that there was a time when I was a person who appreciated a certain amount of discretion in the matter of my public image, a time in which making decisions about my own life felt a bit like contemplating murder, a time when allowing any other person to see my body felt like inviting a detective to arrest me.

We know, of course, that William Shatner was well-known for wearing lifts, and a toupee, and following joyless studio diets to keep his weight down, and spent the majority of his post-sixties career acknowledging and apologizing for himself, at least on-screen if not in his memoirs. I'm not sure that it was ever strictly correct to call myself a closeted trans man. I think as soon as I knew I was one, or wanted to be one, or that one was pretty much the same thing as the other, I told somebody else about it. But a closeted trans man might experience a certain type of transmasculine resonance, watching that scene play out (your transmasculine resonance may vary; transmasculine resonance not guaranteed).

It should perhaps go without saying that unless you are Kevin Pollak, I do not want to hear your William Shatner impression, but I will say it nonetheless, in case you are ever tempted. You might practice your Shatner in the privacy of your own home until your speaking voice becomes indistinguishable from his and you baffle your own ears, and find strange new depths in your own throat. Call me then, but not before.

Most *Columbo* murderers fall into one of two categories. They're either profoundly irritated at his quiet, relentless presence, or they are overwhelmed with relief when he turns up and they can stop trying to run for cover, and find excuses to spend more time with him. He is a rumpled little conscience in an overcoat who dogs their footsteps almost from the moment the murder is completed. There's a moral lightness and an untroubled heart at the core of him, an innate goodness that resonates outward and either puts people immediately at ease or deeply unsettles them, according to the state of their own conscience. Columbo is perhaps the only fictional detective one can imagine sleeping soundly at night. William

Shatner plays the second kind of murderer. The sight of Columbo is an enormous relief to him, a source of joy and freedom from something terrible, and he spends the majority of the second act smiling ruefully at Peter Falk as if to say, "Isn't this all a little ridiculous? Aren't I more than a little ridiculous? Do you want to have lunch with me anyway?" and breaking my heart in the meantime. William Shatner could put a promise into a smile like nobody's business.

There is a website called Shatner's Toupee that—surprisingly uncruelly, given its name—celebrates the quality of *sheepishness* that Shatner brings to *Columbo*. (Sheepishness [n.]: "Affected by or showing embarrassment caused by consciousness of a fault.") Shatner on-screen is always affected, always conscious of the embarrassment he causes others, always conscious of his faults; sheepishness is the fastest way to convince me something or someone is worth loving. Hello, yes I'm very aware that I'm like this, I'm sorry.

It's a very good episode, especially if you are interested, as I am, in watching the breakdown and failure of boyish charm. The last of Shatner's boyishness had left him by about 1976, and "Fade in to Murder" pays it appropriate tribute. His last line to Falk, after a brief and gentle confrontation, is very endearing, and very boyish, and very sad: "Lieutenant," he says, "you'd be doing me an enormous favor if you stopped calling me 'Sir.'" There is no shit-eating in his grin then.

Please don't mistake that ending, or Bill's performance, for sadness. There is no possibility for true sadness in any performance of Bill Shatner's. I don't mean he is not capable of *displaying* sadness, merely that the gigantic reality of his underlying joy can never truly be compromised. Ward Fowler may go to prison, but Columbo has *seen* him first, and that is something no one can take away from him.

A while back I was at a conference in Tennessee with a bunch of medievalists trying to explain something about boyishness, and what it feels like to want to resist it and to drown in it at the same time. We were talking about Apollo and Hyacinthus (I am often, almost always, trying to talk about Apollo and Hyacinthus), and I was trying to figure out why exactly it felt so important to me, once again to explain the connection between the death of Hyacinthus and Ultimate Frisbee. Not because that was *funny*, but because it seemed very important to identify just what kind of beautiful boy he had been (*Are you up? If so, do you want to play Frisbee and die for each other?*). "There is a certain type of beautiful boy who plays Ultimate Frisbee and invites you to come watch his game," I said, "not because he is vain and self-centered, although he maybe is, but because it is the only way he knows how to invite someone to share in his particular joy, and I think maybe the only thing I have ever wanted is to be a very beautiful, very dead, gentle boy that everyone gathers around and looks at." William Shatner was, in his prime, a very beautiful, very gentle boy, although being dead had very little to do with his particular type of boyishness. It was a type of boyishness that drew scrutiny and criticism in a manner much like girlishness, and that seemed to require a constant public apology from him for aging.

I am also firmly of the belief that Captain James T. Kirk was, and is, at every age and in every incarnation, a beautiful lesbian; I fear that now I will be called upon to explain myself and that I will be unable to do so. I can only repeat myself with increasing fervor: *James T. Kirk is a beautiful lesbian, do not ask me any follow-up questions.* Like Goldwater, in your heart you know I'm right. There is plenty of stupid, surface-level evidence I could marshal forth in defense of my argument—people criticized Shatner for his weight, and women are often criticized for their weight; Shatner was beautiful in a way that women are generally beautiful; James T. Kirk lives with her longtime girlfriend (Spock) and her ex-girlfriend (Bones) in a benevolent feelings-and-sex-triad and generally observed the campsite rule when it came to bringing short-term partners around; James T. Kirk is vulnerable and anxious and riddled with sincerity and in love with her car; James T. Kirk wears motorcycle boots and seems to spend a lot of time on her hair, doesn't want kids and rereads Dickens and doesn't feel comfortable showing her feelings in front of anyone she's known less than ten years but that doesn't mean she won't do it—but those things aren't really what make James T. Kirk a beautiful lesbian, I don't think. (It should perhaps go without saying that the contemporary interpreter of Kirk, Chris Pine, is also a beautiful lesbian, but that doesn't have anything to do with my feelings for William Shatner, so we're not going to address that any further here.)

I tried to explain to those same medievalists the strange reaction I have every time I read anything more than one hundred years old. "I feel a profound sense of triumph and superiority over the author," I said, "because they are foolish enough to be dead, while I am young and gloriously alive. Not because I think their *ideas* are outdated or anything like that. It has nothing to do with how they think, or how we see the world differently. It is visceral, it is personal, it is gleeful, and it is triumphant. I have the good sense to still be living, while they have very foolishly died, and it always takes me at least ten minutes to stop crowing over my victory and pay attention to what I am reading." No one else at the table, it turned out, felt quite the same way when reading something by a dead author, but that does not mean I am alone.

William Shatner would have made an excellent Maggie the Cat, because he is *alive*, no matter how many discuses you try to throw at him, no matter how easily the rest of us get distracted by his hairline or his age. He is beautiful, and alive, and *not dead*, and I don't think I've done a very good job explaining anything today.

Rilke Takes a Turn

We cannot fathom his mysterious head
Through the veiled eyes no flickering ray is sent;
But from his torso gleaming light is shed
As from a candelabrum; inward bent

His glance there glows and lingers. Otherwise
The round breast would not bind you with its grace,
Nor could the soft-curved circle of the thighs
Steal the arc whence issues a new race.

Nor could this stark and stunted stone display
Vibrance beneath the shoulders heavy bar,
Nor shine like fur upon a beast of prey,

Nor break forth from its lines like a great star—
There is no spot that does not bind you fast
And transport you back. You should have taken
a left turn at Albuquerque.

Hey, Doc, you've got a slight problem.
Just between the two of us, it's duck-hunting season.

Have you ever had the feeling you were being watched?
Like the eyes of strange things are upon you?
Look, out there in the audience. My,
I bet you monsters lead interesting lives.

I said to my girlfriend just the other day—Gee,
I'll bet monsters are interesting,
I said. The places you must go and the places
you must see, my stars! And I'll bet
you meet a lot of interesting people, too. I'm always
interested in meeting interesting people. You should have taken
a left turn at Albuquerque.

CHAPTER 12

Duckie from *Pretty in Pink* Is Also a Beautiful Lesbian and I Can Prove It with the Intensity of My Feelings

I'm not especially interested in parsing out which of the fictional teenagers should have dated the other fictional teenagers in the movie *Pretty in Pink*; I don't spend a lot of time thinking about who I should have dated in high school, and I see no reason not to apply the same general air of resignation to Andie, Blane, Steff, and Duckie. They're all in high school! They can date everyone in a variety of constellations; they have time for whatever.

I don't know if you care about John Hughes movies. You may not. It may interest you to know that almost every John Hughes movie is about lesbians except for, perhaps unsurprisingly, *Some Kind of Wonderful*. At any rate, *Pretty in Pink* is—correctly, I think—the most beloved of the second-tier Hughes. If you care about any ending to a John Hughes movie, it is probably this one. Here is how the movie ends: Andie (Molly Ringwald) gets together with Blane (Andrew McCarthy), supposedly because the original ending, where she gets together with Duckie (Jon Cryer), didn't test well with audiences.

They would have been a nice couple in a lot of ways. Remarkably ill-suited in others. It would have made him very happy to get to kiss her, and I would have enjoyed seeing him become very happy. (I have no opinion whatsoever on Steff, the character played by James Spader, an insouciance that has always surprised me. I often feel like I ought to have more of a response to James Spader, especially 1980s-era James Spader, but I cannot help how I feel. I do like that he married William Shatner on *Boston Legal*, so I suppose I am inclined to be warmly disposed toward him as a result of the Shatner spillover. And yet.) My primary concern is rescuing Duckie from the slag heap of history, not in determining whether he "ought" to have dated Andie at the end. Most of the Duckie discourse in recent years has centered around whether he is an example of the Nice Guy™, and if so, whether we should all be mad at him for it. My answer is no, for at least two reasons:

1. Duckie seems wholly uninterested in any sort of niceness throughout the course of the movie.
2. Duckie is a lesbian.

Listen, having that one pompadour haircut with a forehead curl, relentless and furiously pining for your best friend, wearing circular sunglasses, hanging out at someone else's job because you don't have anywhere better to be, and being one of the poorest kids in school aren't *necessary preconditions* for lesbianism, but, like, add 'em all up and, baby, you've got a stew going.

There are exactly two Modes of Gay Feeling, no more and no less. Mode of Gay Feeling the first is *Total Domination, How Dare You, I Will Never Die, It Is Impossible for Me to Die, I Thrive On Being Misunderstood.* It's all carefully balanced hats and perfectly styled teddy boy hair and pastel lapels and either having no sex at all or the kind of sex you can't tell your friends about because they're going to get worried for you, and it's wonderful and it's exhausting, and you're funnier than anybody else both because you have to be and because it makes sense and more than a little because you are firmly convinced that a movie crew is always just out of sight recording your entire life and you are playing to the cheap seats, every minute.

Here is the other Mode of Gay Feeling: You still look fantastic, but your stomach hurts and you will never get out of bed. You have learned that rolling your sleeves up over your forearms is very useful to you, sexually speaking, but the person you love and the people you sleep with have absolutely nothing in common, including what they think of your forearms.

I'm not suggesting that Duckie was a lesbian in order to justify whether it was right of him to assume that his being very in love with Andie in any way created an obligation in her to return his feelings; assuredly it wasn't! Assuredly it *isn't*! And yet: how many times in my own life have I thought, wrongly, *The feelings I feel now toward the object of my affections are so blindingly obvious that it is as if I am carrying around the beaming lantern from a lighthouse inside of my chest. How could anyone not notice?* When of course no one *has* noticed.

I'm not saying lesbians have a monopoly on silence, either, not even in the 1980s; there are straight boys who love straight women, probably, and are still reluctant to speak on the subject. But that would have been a good reason, I think, for Duckie not to say anything, yet to feel furious anyhow for not having been understood. It is a hard thing to want to be *interpreted* and not offer anyone a key to the translation.

Is there anything gayer than refusing to ask someone out, then holding them personally responsible for the silent, ever-increasing intensity of your feelings until they tell you casually they're going on a date with someone who asked them out, then exploding with despair? Almost certainly, but no one will tell me what it is.

"I would've died for you" is a complete non sequitur of a response to the sentence "I am going on a date with a boy named Blane," but it's also the only honest thing one *can* say in response. I mean, one shouldn't say it at all, but if one is going to, seventeen is the last acceptable age. This sentiment, by the way, is at least 25 percent of the reason why Bruno Mars is also a lesbian; if you are not a lesbian at the beginning of writing a song as histrionic and self-pitying as "Grenade," you certainly are by the end of it. (I don't know if Bruno Mars actually wrote the song "Grenade." Don't crowd me, kid, I'm just getting warmed up.)

The fact that Duckie's most memorable scene involves fervent, furious lip-synching feels almost *too* on the nose. She bursts into the record store where Andie and the wonderful Iona (Annie Potts) work, disrupting everything, but she does so *in perfect silence*. It's a beautiful performance of total frustration—she's exhausted by the end of it, drooping and spent—and she doesn't sing a single word, doesn't make a single sound. She throws herself to the ground over and over, and she also wears a bolo tie. Of course one can certainly watch Duckie in that scene (and Andie's resultant confusion and panic) as the tantrum of a boy who has mistaken owning a lot of hats for emotional sensitivity, who demands too much time and energy and attention from the women around him, you absolutely can. Probably John Hughes did.

You can also watch that scene as the tantrum of a lesbian who has mistaken owning a lot of hats for emotional sensitivity, who demands too much from others; just because I think Duckie is a lesbian doesn't mean that she is making excellent and healthy choices. Duckie twitches around afterward like a hummingbird, as if her hands stopped moving around in emphatic gestures for even a second they might betray her into giving something away. But I recommend watching that scene, focusing as much as you can on Iona's face throughout. She sees something she recognizes, wants to hail in *direct acknowledgment,* and also challenge. I think that thing she recognizes is a particular sort of lesbian sadness, and I want to recognize it, too, even though it's not exactly mine.

Before I started testosterone I bought myself a lot of cheap accessories, both as a distraction and at least partly in the hope they would weigh me down and provide me with an actual, physical sense of being grounded. I went into a secondhand store on my way to the supermarket and I hailed the woman behind the front desk. "I want to buy at least eight silver rings from you," I said, and did exactly that. It was absolutely wonderful, and she was as happy for me as I was.

There was a ninth ring that I did not buy, because things were getting a little ridiculous, and the woman behind the counter said, "Tell you what. I'll put it to the side, and if you can't stop thinking about it, you come back." There are so many things I can't stop thinking about! And so many places I find myself going back to! Aren't things getting a little ridiculous?

My girlfriend, Grace, before she was my girlfriend, was working on an article about George Eliot and texted me something Jane Carlyle once wrote about Eliot:

> I hope to know someday if the person I am addressing bears any resemblance in external things to the idea I have conceived of [them] in my mind. . . . How ridiculous all this may read beside the reality.

I texted back, "I identify strongly with ending the description of a fervent, cherished wish with 'how ridiculous.' I love you, Jane Carlyle. Also I just bought eight rings."

"It really is pretty sweet," my friend texted back, "given how awful she was."

Duckie might have been awful but I can forgive her, because she was awfully sweet, too, and I wish I could do more to help her.

I Have a Friend Who Thinks Umbrellas Are Enemies of the Collective Good, and I Have a Sneaking Suspicion They May Be Right

She's from England, I mean *England* England; it's true to say that she's from the UK, and it's also true to say that she's from England—both things are true of her—and I had no idea she felt that way about umbrellas until the first time we got caught in the rain together and I offered to share my umbrella with her and she said, "I don't believe in umbrellas."

Which no one had ever said to me before, and it made me a little worried because I realized I was going to have trouble guessing things she would want to hear me say and then saying them, not necessarily because I meant them but because I wanted to please, which was something I did a lot without admitting it to myself. I was surprised and I said, "What's not to believe in?"

She said: "An umbrella keeps you dry by diverting all the water to roll away from you and onto other people. It's an enemy of the collective good and I'd rather just wear a raincoat." So we didn't share an umbrella that day, or any day thereafter, even though we've been caught in the rain an awful lot since then.

A couple of things have changed since I wrote this title; she's no longer my *friend-who-goes-by-they* but my girlfriend-who-goes-by-she. We live together, and shortly after we moved in I found an umbrella in the front hall closet. When I asked her about it, she said, "I think I got it from my last roommate," then pursed her lips together and added, "Needless to say, you've never seen me use it," which is another thing that's true about her.

CHAPTER 13

Sir Gawain Just Wants to Leave Castle Make-Out

Wherein I finally learn that leaving parties early, failing to cope, and pulling an Irish exit on first dates puts me in excellent literary company.

KING ARTHUR: it's Christmas so anyone who wants to
    come to my house and absolutely scream at me is
    entirely welcome to do so
GREEN KNIGHT: hi hi hi, merry Christmas, look at my
    neck!
    (it's green)
    (that's not all of me that's green ;))
    come over
    it'll be fun
    let's cut each other's heads off with swords or this axe
GAWAIN: what
GREEN KNIGHT: you can make out with my wife
GAWAIN: sorry what
GREEN KNIGHT: you can make out with me
GAWAIN: what?

GREEN KNIGHT: look just come over
  we'll have dinner, with all of our heads on, and also
    wearing clothes
  you hit me today and I'll hit you a year from now
GAWAIN: it's *Christmas*
GREEN KNIGHT: fine
  hit me today and I'll hit you next year the day after
    Christmas
  happy?
GAWAIN: I don't understand the rules of this game
  or the prize
  what is the goal here
GREEN KNIGHT: are you going to cut my head off or what

[*GAWAIN cuts off the GREEN KNIGHT's head*]

GREEN KNIGHT: fantastic, thank you
  see you in a year

[*The GREEN KNIGHT picks up his head and rides away*]

GAWAIN: oh my God
KING ARTHUR: honestly
  my advice to you is to not even worry about this
GUINEVERE: yeah
  do not take this seriously
GAWAIN: but what will I do next year when it is his turn
    to—
KING ARTHUR: look
  i just said that was my advice

[*One year later*]

GREEN KNIGHT: welcome to my castle, we've definitely
never cut off each other's heads before, my name is
Bertilak and I am a regular human color, how are you

GAWAIN: thank you for your hospitality, but I cannot stay
long

I have an appointment with a man at the Green Chapel
in a few days

GREEN KNIGHT: the Green Chapel is JUST down the
road from here, probably

you should just stay here until your appointment, stay
here with me and my wife

GAWAIN: very well, I accept

GREEN KNIGHT: oh but shoot

I have to go on a hunt, like *right* now

so why don't we just agree to play a game for as long as
you're staying here

where I bring you whatever I find outside during the day

and you bring me whatever you find in my own house
during the day

GAWAIN: what an odd suggestion

why don't I just come hunting with you instead?

GREEN KNIGHT: NO

no, you just stay here in the castle and give me whatever
you find at the end of every day

GAWAIN: but you already own everything in the castle, it's
yours

GREEN KNIGHT: I WILL SEE YOU ON THE MORROW

LADY BERTILAK: whatcha kissin'

GAWAIN: hm?

oh, nothing

LADY BERTILAK: let's make out

GAWAIN: I don't feel like we should do that

LADY BERTILAK: if you don't kiss me at least once it would really hurt my feelings

GAWAIN: well
if it would hurt your feelings

LADY BERTILAK: fantastic, thank you!
now you can make out with my husband tonight

GREEN KNIGHT: GAWAIN
I have brought you a deer from today's hunt
what do you have for me

GAWAIN: I, uh
I guess I have some kissing for you to have

GREEN KNIGHT: sounds great
[*They kiss*]
okay, see you tomorrow

GAWAIN: oh I really don't want to play this game again, this is making me sort of unco—

GREEN KNIGHT: tomorrow!!

LADY BERTILAK: let's have sex

GAWAIN: Okay, no for two reasons
first you are my host's wife and that goes against every vow of knighthood ever
and the second half is that then I would also have to have sex with your husband
according to your weird castle sex game

LADY BERTILAK: mm that sounds like a Gawain problem not a Lady Bertilak problem

GAWAIN: well I'm not having sex with you

LADY BERTILAK: fine
here's my underwear though, you have to take it
otherwise it would be rude

GAWAIN: well

I don't want to be rude

excuse me, I have to go kiss your husband again

GREEN KNIGHT: Well, Gawain,

it's been a great time here at Castle Make-Out

but you'd probably better go fight that Green Knight you
keep talking about

GAWAIN: I will certainly perish when it is his turn to deliver
the blow

Farewell, friend

GREEN KNIGHT: Gawain

Gawain it was me the whole time

GAWAIN: what

GREEN KNIGHT: I'm the same guy, from before

only I'm not gonna kill you

I'm just gonna fuck up your neck a little because you
kept my wife's underwear and didn't tell me

but you're all right, guy

you're all right

GAWAIN: what the hell

what the hell was the point of any of this

why the hell did you set all this up for

GREEN KNIGHT: :)

GAWAIN: what the HELL

KNIGHTS OF THE ROUND TABLE: henceforth we shall
all wear green sashes

to celebrate the valuable lesson we have learned this
day

GAWAIN: WHAT LESSON

WHAT THE HELL HAPPENED

KNIGHTS OF THE ROUND TABLE: :)

PART II

In the fairy tale an incomprehensible happiness rests upon an incomprehensible condition. A box is opened, and all evils fly out. A word is forgotten, and cities perish. A lamp is lit, and love flies away. A flower is plucked, and human lives are forfeited. An apple is eaten, and the hope of God is gone. . . . To be breakable is not the same as to be perishable. Strike a glass, and it will not endure an instant; simply do not strike it, and it will endure a thousand years. Such, it seemed, was the joy of man, either in elfland or on earth; the happiness depended on NOT DOING SOMETHING which you could at any moment do and which, very often, it was not obvious why you should not do.

    —G. K. Chesterton, "The Ethics of Elfland," *Orthodoxy*

"Begad," said the green knight, "Sir Gawain, I am pleased to find from thy fist the favor I asked for!"

    —Sir Gawain and the Green Knight,
    translated by J. R. R. Tolkien

It's difficult not to read the Pearl Poet's *Sir Gawain and the Green Knight* without envisioning a sort of Benny Hill–style montage of hot-potato sexual tension: Lady Bertilak chasing Sir Gawain around the castle trying to stuff girdles and rings in his pocket; Sir Gawain running full-tilt away from her with his fingers stuffed in his ears, listing women he's disliked; Lord Bertilak throwing open a series of doors with a hopeful expression and making out with whoever's behind them. The account the *Green Knight* gives of kissing, of giving kisses, of asking to be kissed, seemed as sound an account as any to me, who found the concept fascinating but the practice baffling and impenetrable. The best and strongest men in the world are all assembled together; who that loved men would not ride into that hall and beg one of them to cut off your head? And who has ever been injured by men and not been disappointed at the insufficiency of the wound afterward? *Come over, but don't stay over; look at me, but not like that; here, trade kisses with someone else who will act as my emissary—now what on earth did you go and kiss her for?*—the game of bodies and beheading made very little sense as a trans person who had no language for the way I experienced my body or the bodies of others, no way to explain that I could imagine myself as a girl and I could imagine myself being kissed if I worked hard enough at it, but never both at the same time. *Welcome to my house, now you have to kiss both of us* made as much sense as any other set of rules about kissing I'd ever been offered.

The closest I could ever come to imagining a romantic interaction that would need to acknowledge the body was this: I would imagine myself at the local dairy where some of my friends had part-time jobs. A stranger would rush in and shoot me, wounding me mortally but not immediately killing me, then just as immediately depart. My friends would gather round in horror and pity, all wishing they had loved me better and admiring the beautiful, gallant way in which I prepared to meet death. I would say bravely that my final wish was not to die unkissed, and one of my friend's boyfriends would solemnly and respectfully oblige; then I would die and the fantasy would restart, possibly with a new outfit. This had the benefit of infusing every hypothetical kiss with the urgency of the grave, while simultaneously freeing me from having to imagine what on earth might be expected of me *after* kissing, or worse, what asking to be kissed without the threat of death might look like. Had I had access to a phrase like "transmasculine resonance" at a younger age I might have found a certain transmasculine resonance in Sir Gawain trapped in somebody else's house trying to avoid kisses from both men and women while worrying about unavoidable physical challenges and the threat of blood; as it was I instead developed a habit of leaving parties abruptly, usually after saying, "I'm going to the bathroom, I'll be back in a minute."

When I was just teetering on the verge of puberty, between sixth and seventh grade (I say teetering but this was the midnineties and everyone was still drinking that bad milk with all the hormones in it instead of the healthful modern raw milk that sometimes kills you, so I probably had a solid two or three years of menstruation under my belt at that point) I spent a lot of time on the bus ride home from school listening to the classic-rock station. This was for two reasons; the first was that none of my friends were on my bus line until eighth grade, and the second was that I didn't own a Walkman until high school. There were a couple of songs popular on the suburban Chicago classic-rock station that seemed designed to introduce a white eleven-year-old to the idea of the blues as gradually as possible: Melissa Etheridge's "I'm the Only One," Marc Cohn's "Walking in Memphis," and a smattering of Bonnie Raitt, all of which played on absolutely constant rotation. I was very preoccupied with the idea that I was never going to go on a date or be kissed, an idea I found both desolating and incredibly romantic, and they served as the ideal accompanying soundtrack for planning a sexy, sexless future. They turned out to be, in fact, relatively formative when it came to my idea of what sexy women sounded like and thought about. The best possible future I could envision for myself (while remaining realistic—it was one thing to imagine myself dying heroically at Oberweis Dairy while my friend Katie's boyfriend honorably kissed me into the grave, but quite another to imagine myself trapped with a boyfriend of my own) looked a lot like soft-rock-infused yearning solitude. I could imagine myself as a grown woman only in total isolation from the rest of humanity, and believed the absolute sexiest thing a grown woman could be was "incredibly sad about Elvis," just like Alannah Myles in "Black Velvet."

Perhaps it would have been better for me if I could have seen the movie *Velvet Goldmine* or heard of the Smiths at that age instead, and transitioned at fourteen. I might have called myself Trenton and had a cis boyfriend at fifteen; I might even today be five foot ten instead of five foot seven and a half inches tall. But I did not have access to *Velvet Goldmine* or the Smiths; I had access to Alannah Myles and Sir Gawain and church and was going to have to make do with what I had. By the time I *did* encounter *Velvet Goldmine* and the Smiths I had already developed various strategies of self-protection, and was mostly safe from becoming unbearable about them. I wanted male romantic attention very badly, and couldn't stand it at the same time; I briefly had a boyfriend in college and spent almost every night of the week going over to his house, flirting outrageously with him, then sneaking out the window to avoid spending the night, feeling as I drove home every time that I had just pulled off the most marvelous escape, while simultaneously missing him already.

> The Green Knight on the ground now gets himself ready,
> leaning a little with the head he lays bare the flesh,
> and his locks long and lovely he lifts over his crown,
> letting the naked neck as was needed appear.
> His left foot on the floor before him placing,
> Gawain gripped on his ax, gathered and raised it,
> from aloft let it swiftly land where 'twas naked,
> so that the sharp of his blade shivered the bones,
> and sank clean through the clear fat and clove it asunder,
> and the blade of the bright steel then bit into the ground.
> The fair head to the floor fell from the shoulders,
> and folk fended it with their feet as forth it went rolling;
> the blood burst from the body, bright on the greenness,
> and yet neither faltered nor fell the fierce man at all,
> but stoutly he strode forth, still strong on his shanks,

and roughly he reached out among the rows that stood there,
caught up his comely head and quickly upraised it,
and then hastened to his horse, laid hold of the bridle,
stepped into stirrup-iron, and strode up aloft,
his head by the hair in his hand holding;
and he settled himself then in the saddle as firmly
as if unharmed by mishap, though in the hall he might wear
no head.
His trunk he twisted round,
that gruesome body that bled,
and many fear then found,
as soon as his speech was sped.

To force a roomful of men to admire your ability to withstand physical pain and visibly bleeding ax wound—it may be that there is such a thing as *too* much transmasculine resonance, and better for me that I would not come to know of it for years and years. If you're bewildered by that, boys, you should come visit my castle and meet my wife sometime!

I don't think it's quite correct to say that I didn't feel like transition was possible at all, much less for me, until I came to know trans men. It's still less correct to say that I transitioned *for* trans men, not just because of them, and yet something about that statement seems true however much I might want to resist it. I don't quite know how to acknowledge that truth without creating a separate, wholly sovereign category for trans men that can serve as lazy shorthand for "men, but good" or "men, but not really—well, yes of course, *trans men are men!* but not like *that*," or, worst of all, "men, but safe, due to perceived dicklessness." Anything that frames trans men as a sort of Skipper to cis men's Barbie seems rooted more in wishful or even delusional thinking than in reality, and elfland never tolerates wishful thinking. But the point remains that my whole young life I carried around a great and a secret love for men I did not feel safe expressing *to* men, because they could not be trusted with the love I—foolishly, impulsively, unwillingly—had for them; when I began to know trans men later in my life, regardless of whether I found them variously attractive, boring, self-centered, passive-aggressive, badly dressed, charming, clingy, or rude, I was at last ready to set my love down and offer it, to name it with full confidence in the middle of a great hall. I'd been so in love with boys and never told any of them, and I was so ready to say so out loud, and so ashamed, I could burst.

But not knowing my other options, Alannah Myles was the best kind of woman I could imagine myself becoming—too in love with a single dead boy to go out with any of the alive boys who might be interested in her, which seemed like a pretty reasonable position for a grown woman to take, I thought as an eleven-year-old with two solid years of menstruation under his belt. I needed boys to leave me alone so that I could be properly alone with boys. Sexy women stood on porches wailing about Elvis and wearing full chaps over their jeans, and the most billowing white shirts imaginable; maybe someday I could be so sexy that men would pay attention to me but never get close enough to remind me that I had a body.

It's a genuinely great and, I think, truly funny song; the moment the music stops to reflect on just how sad it was that Elvis *died*—"In a flash he was gone—it happened so soon," Myles sings, shaking her head mournfully and lapsing into a respectful silence. Elvis is *DEAD* and *that's* why I can't go out with you tonight. Of course, any eleven-year-old's idea of what adult sexiness looks like is bound to be ridiculous. And there was something funny too, in being thirty years old and throwing a tantrum in my therapist's office about how I didn't *want* to want to be a boy because boys weren't going to be *nice* to me. The rules of elfland are always bewildering, but that's never stopped anyone from wandering in before.

No One Understands
Henry VIII Like I Do

One of the biggest hypothetical problems when it comes to transitioning is that it really fouls up your time-travel fantasies, or at least muddles them for a good long while. (Another problem is whether to refer to transition as a *sex change*, which I've seen a handful of people do for a variety of reasons. There's something pleasingly retro about it, but I'm not quite sure I'm tall enough to pull that style off. *Transition* it is, at least for now.) I've always felt particularly *prepared* for time travel, to be in a position where I would be forced to keep my head down, abandon my values for expediency, and say only things I knew other people wanted to hear in order to survive.

There's no transmasculine equivalent of forced-femme fantasy ("HELPLESS college freshman FORCED into a pullover and called LITTLE BUDDY by older brother's COOL BEST FRIEND: BECOMING A BOY FOR MALE ATTENTION"), at least not that I ever came across, so my daydreams always took the shape of being forced to travel back in time to an era where I'd finally have to be a woman as hard and as long as I could. The plan was always (after stepping through a ley line or mysterious portal): keep my head down, wait for other people to start talking before opening my mouth and giving myself away with an out-of-place accent or vocabulary, agree with everything I'm told instead of trying to advocate for modern behavioral standards, look for context clues, start a lot of conversations with, "Oh, hello, you," get a low-level job and act so normal for decades that everyone leaves me alone, respond in kind to anyone who refers to me as "darling," immediately stop making references to air travel or television or anything that might sound like magic (if in the future, refuse to ask "What does this do?" about anything), immediately abandon every single value of my own for contemporary ones so that whatever this culture approves of, I approve of, and whatever this culture abhors, so do I, make no waves, ask no questions, come up with a decent explanation for my clothing before getting changed as quickly as possible, let other idiots try to avert the Battle of Hastings or invent feminism eight hundred years early or whatever, and either get home safely or find a way to live as comfortably as possible. The most cherished and longstanding of these counterproductive fantasies involves the court of Henry VIII.

The really nice thing about imagining yourself as a wife of Henry VIII is that you got to deal with every single male authority figure imaginable all at once, because he was everybody's god and pope and dad and husband and boss, so if you wanted to fight or resent or betray or fuck or suck up to any one of them you could get it all done at once with the same very tall person. Moreover, I had the benefit of hindsight and knew that his daughter Elizabeth I would later invent feminism, so I didn't need to feel guilty about abandoning mine for her father, or for never imagining myself accidentally time-traveled to her court.

I knew enough about the futility of changing a man (or worse, trying to change a man in order to try to change myself) that I thought it best to confine such fantasies to the distant past. Henry VIII married everyone in the home counties, invented Christmas music, and was winning enough to make Anne Boleyn swim across the Channel to introduce the blow job to England; both sufficiently charismatic and sufficiently dead to hang a lifetime of maladaptive fantasies on. It's easy, with the benefit of hindsight and roughly two television specials per year, to feel superior to Catherine of Aragon. Twenty-four years spent in the company of God's representative on earth, yet that still somehow wasn't enough time for her to learn that he was as easily soothed as he was irritated. Henry was a simple man: he wanted literally everyone to love him without reserve or criticism, and he believed God invented England so he could have sons in it. That was it; that was the one thing to remember about him. When the king of England, who has been trying to divorce you for years, offers you the chance to say, "My lord! I see now what a mistake I have made, and that I have never truly been your lawful wife. I see it all now! I must have consummated my marriage with Arthur and forgotten, and consider you my dear brother, and will never bother you again with an attempt to assert my wifely rights," you say it with a smile on your face and accept your consolation castle in Coventry. Stick to your guns, and where does it get you? A handful of servants who were willing to call you the queen, a hair shirt, and nothing, plus whenever they make movies about Queen Elizabeth they always make up the actress who plays your daughter Mary to look like a nightmare.

The problem with all these fantasies now—not that Catherine of Aragon would have ever welcomed advice from me at any age, in any form, and obviously Henry VIII would have been lousy at helping me get into a pullover—is how to explain a transitioning body to the friendly peasant woman I assume will lend me a cloak and a loaf of fresh brown bread after I stumble disheveled and disoriented out of the Portal; I have enough trouble passing in 2019 Berkeley, California, without wondering how I'm going to get read by early modern courtiers. But the fantasy persists, and there are at least two reasons why the Tudors are such an important component of it: One, because it helps to make obvious the ridiculousness of similar questions that try to pass themselves off as legitimate concerns, like "What if you start to transition and then society collapses, and you're *artificially dependent* on something society provides for you, like hormones?" The answer to that, of course, is that if society collapses, I'll die and so will you, even if you have a second freezer and some MREs in your basement and know how to do push-ups. I am artificially dependent on everything from electricity to antibiotics to refrigeration and indoor plumbing. Taking up the hobby of survivalism will not extend my life another five minutes past the end of human civilization, and there's no good reason to put off present happiness, usefulness, and meaning to prop up the fantasy of being able to survive without depending on anybody else.

The second reason the Tudors are important is because the backdrop I choose for my maladaptive fantasies tells me something about what I'm not prepared to articulate or ask for myself. Put me back in time where gender roles were *more* strictly enforced, give me a body I've got to account for to some greater authority every second of the day, throw me into a high-stakes fertility-and-death cult centered around the tallest man in England and keep me sufficiently distracted with high stakes and high demands and let me get the job of fulfilling an unpleasant man's expectations *done*. I suppose the real problem is—as it's always been—that once you bring up the possibility of time travel in relation to transition, the natural first stop is going to be puberty, not the Tudor court, to increase the possibilities available to one's own future rather than restrict all options outside of "giving an heir to Henry VIII." But if you look at the past just right, you can almost picture it.

CHAPTER 14

"I Love Your Vibe," and Other Things I've Said to Men

S omething I used to do in my life as a woman was to occasionally, and under very controlled circumstances, shout encouragingly at groups of young men on the street, like "WHAT WOULD YOU SAY IS YOUR FAVORITE MONTH OF THE YEAR IF YOU HAD TO PICK ONE?" or "I LIKE THAT YOU ALL HAVE DIFFERENT-COLORED SHORTS ON, YOU SEEM LIKE YOU HAVE A REALLY FUN FRIENDSHIP DYNAMIC," or "I HOPE YOUR NIGHT IS MAGICAL, AND DON'T LET COACH HASSLE YOU TOO MUCH." Invariably their reaction would be one of astonishment and delight, and I treasured it, although it did not stop other men from occasionally saying things to me on the street I did not particularly like hearing. I had a sense that whatever I was getting out of this, whatever function this habit was performing in my life, had an expiration date, and the last time I shouted across the street to a man I didn't know was a few months before I started transition. I'd been driving around Oakland with a friend of mine one night and we spotted a cyclist across the street waiting for the light to change. Lots of cyclists in Oakland wear headlamps at night, but this one was completely Tronned out: his entire bike, his jacket, even his backpack were outlined in green and blue LED lights, but the best part was his helmet, which slowly changed colors every few seconds. I was about to make an unprotected left, and I rolled down the passenger-side window and shouted, "I LOVE YOUR VIBE" as we passed him, only I wasn't sure that he heard me because it was a relatively noisy intersection and I didn't want to yell too loudly and distract him.

Later on—we were just cruising around, not going anywhere in particular—we saw the same cyclist again about to cross a different street in front of us, and my friend said, "You should tell him that you like his vibe again, because I'm not sure he heard you the first time." I couldn't bring myself to do it again, even though I *did* love his vibe, and I *did* want him to know it, and I wished I could have told him.

"I don't want to yell too much," I said, "and I don't want to distract him when he's trying to cross the street, and I definitely don't want to say it when I'm stuck behind a red light and can't drive off." So I didn't yell anything, and eventually I took my friend home, and then I went home, too.

I never did yell at groups of men very often. Conditions had to be perfect, and I wanted to make sure I never did it where somebody might look up suddenly in surprise and get hit by a car while they were trying to cross against traffic, or when they were in the middle of a serious or painful conversation, because hollering ought to be offered judiciously. But it was important to me, maybe crucial to me, because the moment of bewilderment always gave way to joy in a sequence I was never able to re-create in any other area of my life. I wanted very much for men always to be gently delighted, even though they so rarely were, and I wanted always to be the one surprising and delighting them. I was also of course aware that this was not the normal order of operations when stuff gets yelled on the street and groups of men are involved, but that didn't stop me from wishing all men were on bikes and beautifully lit up and riding around changing colors, and that the rest of us could all tell them how much we loved their vibes, and that I was always driving my friends home at the end of a really good night.

I think it's also good not to yell at anybody, and that it's probably better not to yell at all than to try to change the dynamic of public yelling.

It was around that same time that I spent most of my days working out of a coffee shop near my apartment. There was a jaunty sort of barista there who once came out from behind the counter to talk to me about my shoes with the most undisguised, unselfconscious joy and ever after that conversation we would have the following back-and-forth when I came into the shop:

PEACEFUL MALE BARISTA: Hey, man!
SELF, GLOWING AND TERRIFIED: Oh, hey, man!
PMB: How's it going?
SG&T: Awesome, awesome. [Or alternately: Great, great.]
PMB: What shoes do you have on today?
SG&T: These ones!
PMB: Oh, nice, so nice for *sure.*
SG&T: Right on, right on, for sure.
PMB: Thanks, man!

Sometimes I called him "sir" or "young squire" and he seemed to really get a kick out of that. I got a real kick out of it, too. I hope he has a drum kit, or plans to get a drum kit someday.

Whenever I see a pack of young guns out on the street who seem like they're having a good time with one another—I mean really seem to enjoy one another's company, and know how to be

in a group together well, and have figured out the line between joyful ribbing and straight-up hassling, and delight in the former and
eschew the latter, the kinds of dudes who are mostly big headphones
and big shoes and backpacks and ears and friendliness—part of me
really believes that if I ran up to them and said hello, their square-
boy, gung ho faces would light up with recognition and delight and
they'd say, "Oh, hey, man! Hey, man, it's so good to see you! We
were wondering where you were at. We're so glad you're here, man."
And then we'd all walk around together, and maybe try to see if the
Denny's by the overpass was open twenty-four hours or if it was the
other Denny's that was open for twenty-four hours, and we'd drive
around until it was time to go home.

House Hunters

MAN: We have come to buy nothing.

WOMAN: We are here to buy NOTHING.

REALTOR: I stand as witness! Here is NOTHING.

MAN: NOTHING. GIVE US NOTHING.

WOMAN: FILL OUR HANDS AND MOUTHS WITH NOTHING.

MAN: THERE IS A WARM CAT THAT DWELLS IN MY HEART AND BATS AWAY MY THOUGHTS. HE MAKES ME DIZZY. I WOULD HATE HIM IF I COULD.

WOMAN: I. I. I. I PROHIBIT CLOSETS. I ABJURE THE ENHANGMENT OF CLOTHES. I BANISH THE BARRIERS BETWEEN DOOR AND WALL, BETWEEN SCONCE AND HALL. I WILL SLEEP IN MY OWN HANDSHAKE.

REALTOR: I REFUSE TO PRODUCE. I COME GIFT-LESS. I COME OFFERLESS.

MAN: PUT ME NOWHERE. LIST MY ADDRESS AS *NULL*.

WOMAN: NULL.

REALTOR: NULL.

HOUSE HUNTERS II

WOMAN: [*angrily*] We told you not to bring us inside of a
house to visit. Our budget was nullification, wrack,
and slaughter. I am *enwalled*. Get us out at once.

REALTOR: [*trapped outside on a ledge*] I am sorry. I am
sorry. I don't know how this happened. The house
has chosen us, I think. I had no part in this.

WOMAN: YOU MAY NOT WASH YOUR HANDS OF
US. There were no stars the night I was born. I was
born without a sign.

MAN: I feel the neighbors can see me. I fear the neighbors can
see me. I must, I must, I must—[*he becomes impossibly
long and thin, then crawls inside of the crown molding*]

REALTOR: [*slipping, despite herself*] I had a mother once. I
had a nightmare once. Forgive me.

WOMAN: We will buy nothing, spirits! Do you hear us?
Send torment, defeat, ruin—*we came here to purchase
nothing and you will not sway us from our path.* And I
do not forgive you, house-lackey.

MAN: [*weakly, from inside the walls*] I am the house now. I
do not forgive either. ENMITY.

WOMAN: ENMITY.

REALTOR: [*brokenly, resignedly*] Enmity, then. [*She falls.*]

HOUSE HUNTERS II ~~INTERNATIONAL~~

WOMAN: We have traveled long and far, without sleep and
without bread, to tell you this: we do not need two
sinks. We are already drained.

MAN: [*dully, without opening his eyes*] Do not give us two
sinks. I must not—I must not look at the sinks.

WOMAN: [*alarmed*] Do not look at the sinks!

MAN: [*pained, desperate*] I must not look at the sinks!

REALTOR: [*throwing herself across the bathroom counter*]
There are no sinks here! There are no sinks! Brother,
all is well! Brother, all is well! Brother, all is well, and—

MAN: [*shrieking, eyes lidless*]: I MUST NOT LOOK AT
THE *SINKS*.

HOUSE HUNTERS III

*The WOMAN and the REALTOR stand trembling in the BATH-
ROOM. The room is silent. So are they, for a long while.*

REALTOR: Perhaps—

WOMAN: Do not say it.

REALTOR: I only—

WOMAN: *Please.*

REALTOR: I'm sorry.

The WOMAN slides down against the wall and leans against the toilet.

WOMAN: How long, do you think, before the school district arrives? Before we are Zoned?

REALTOR: It does not always come. We may not be Zoned.

WOMAN: Please, now, after all this—do not lie to me. I do
not wish for the last thing you say to me to be a lie.

REALTOR: Everything I have said to you has been a lie.
[*She slides down against the wall as well, and leans
forward until her head is resting upon the WOMAN's
knees.*] If we are not Zoned, we will be Partitioned, or
left to lose our minds in the gibbering emptiness of
the Open Floor Plan, or—

WOMAN: I hope it is not the Walk-In Closet. Perhaps that's weak of me to say. I should not be so afraid, and yet, I fear the Walk-In Closet above all else. Do you think he—[*she jerks her head in the direction of the SINK, which is growing slowly but steadily larger*]—do you think he suffered a great deal?

The REALTOR spreads her hands and smiles helplessly.

WOMAN: Do you think he is still suffering?
REALTOR: *You have asked me not to lie to you.*

The WOMAN begins to cry in earnest this time.

WOMAN: I choose, I choose, I choose—I choose the third house, I *choose* it, I choose the house within walking distance of the shopping district, with the too-small kitchen, with the windowless in-law unit, *I choose, I purchase, I offer, I hunt the house, please.* I have brought this on myself.

The WOMAN idly runs her hands through the REALTOR's hair.

WOMAN: I offer myself as budget. I am willing to—to go over.
REALTOR: I can feel his suffering. Even now.
WOMAN: *I forgive you.*
REALTOR: Do not. Please. [*She retches, but cannot bring herself to vomit.*]

The WOMAN kisses the REALTOR. The REALTOR melts into the kiss and runs a feverish hand along THE WOMAN's jawline.

REALTOR: [*wonderingly, helplessly*] You have such—clean
lines.

*A horrid shuddering sound comes from just outside the BATHROOM
DOOR. The WOMAN and the REALTOR cling to each other. The
SINK gurgles, and a MAN'S HAND emerges from it.*

SINK: NOT TO GO ON ALL FOURS. NOT TO SUCK
UP DRINK. NOT TO CHASE ONE ANOTHER.
ARE WE NOT MEN?
WOMAN: God, God. God, God. God, God.
SINK: HIS IS THE HAND THAT MAKES. HIS IS THE
HAND THAT WOUNDS. HIS IS THE HAND
THAT HEALS.

The MAN's voice joins the SINK's.

MAN: OUR BID HAS BEEN ACCEPTED, DARLING.
WE MUST GO INTO ESCROW. WE MUST SIGN.
YOUR NAME NEXT TO MINE.

*The SHUDDERING SOUND intensifies. The WOMAN buries her
head in the crook of the REALTOR's neck.*

WOMAN: *If you have anything in your pockets—if you have ever
loved me, or him—you will kill me, you will do it now—*
REALTOR: I—

*The DOOR opens. The HAND IN THE SINK waves in greeting.
The REALTOR looks down at what she is holding in her arms, and
screams.*

CHAPTER 15

And His Name Shall Be Called Something Hard to Remember

And He said, "Your name shall no longer be called Jacob, but Israel; for you have struggled with God and with men, and have prevailed."

—Genesis 32:28

And they said to him, *It's not that we don't like the name Israel, it's just that we've always called you Jacob. We're so used to it.*

And he said to them, *Right, no, I get that, I do know that you've always called me by that name before, I hadn't forgotten. I've been used to it, too, ha-ha! And I really appreciate your bearing with me—*

And they said, *Well, first things first, you should definitely know that we're going to get it wrong sometimes.*

And again he said, *Of course! I figured that.*

And they said, *We just really want to stress, before moving on to any other topics, that we're going to forget a lot, and use the old name. That's the first thing we want you to know, now that you've made your request, just how badly we plan on carrying it out.*

And Jacob said, *Okay.*

And they said that a lot. And everyone else said that, too, with astonishing regularity upon hearing the new name, so eventually when Jacob—sorry, *Israel*—told anyone about it he started saying it for them, to save time, *My name shall no longer be called Jacob but Israel for I have struggled with God and with men and have prevailed but I don't expect you to get it right all the time, I know it's a big change, I totally understand that it'll take some time to adjust.*

And some of them said, *What if we came up with a name that meant both? Sort of in between until it feels more natural? Like Isracob or Jasrael. Yeah, we're going to call you Isracob.*

To which Israel said, *I—okay. If you think it'll help.*

And they said, *Thanks for understanding. It's just that this is really hard for us, too, you know? In some ways, it's like you've died.*

To which Israel said, *In which ways?*

And they said, *Please don't get defensive.*

And some of them took "it'll take some time to adjust" as "forever," which had not been what Jacob—Israel! Sorry, sorry, sorry! It's just that my brain is so *used* to saying Jacob, because you really *are* Jacob in my brain, just Jacob-doing-something-weird-these-days—had meant at all.

And some of the others said Israel some of the time, and Jacob some of the time, exclaiming *Oh my God, oh my God!! ISRAEL, sorry, oh my God I'm SO sorry* after each accidental *Jacob* such that each time was more noticeable than the time before, and Israel found himself saying, *It's fine, don't worry about it; it's totally fine, don't feel bad; I didn't even notice; Jacob is fine, I honestly always liked Jacob better anyways.*

CHAPTER 16

Pirates at the Funeral: "It Feels Like Someone Died," but Someone Actually Didn't

A particularly thorny modern question of etiquette is how to properly receive, as an alive person who has recently advertised either an intention to transition or that transition has already begun, any variation on the following sentiment: "It feels like someone died." Sometimes people are willing to be more specific and clarify, "It feels like *you*, the transitioning person, died," or possibly "It feels like my spouse/parent/child/sibling/friend died." But more often than not, I think, non-transitioning people prefer the safety of announcing the death of *Someone* rather than name the transitioner outright. It serves as a softer replacement for "You're dead to me," as the speaker lacks either the desire or the determination to simply announce an estrangement. *It feels like* Someone *died—I won't say who—you know who I'm talking about, the party of the first part—but let's not speak ill of the dead.*

One worries that responding with the good news that one is not dead at all but very much alive—that one is, in fact, moving in the direction of vitality, animation, the future, developing a new kind of continuity, carrying on the good work of naming and identification that all people have been charged with—would not be received with wonder and relief. Yet, like Tom Sawyer listening to his aunt Polly reproach herself after believing him to have drowned, the temptation remains to "rush out from under the bed and overwhelm [them] with joy."

But how to talk someone who loves you out of their grief? One might argue (*I'm not dead, nor anything like it; you're mistaken*), or persuade (*I'll be just around the corner from my own life; come by and visit anytime*), or demand, or manipulate, or threaten, or cajole, try to strike some sort of bargain: *What if I were to transition as little as possible—might my condition be upgraded merely to some sort of serious but nonfatal complaint?* How does one behave as a guest at one's own funeral? Anyone might be naturally curious to see such a thing, if only to luxuriate in how much one is missed. Tom Sawyer and Huckleberry Finn did it to profoundly satisfying effect:

> As the service proceeded, the clergyman drew such pictures of the graces, the winning ways, and the rare promise of the lost lads that every soul there, thinking he recognized these pictures, felt a pang in remembering that he had persistently blinded himself to them always before, and had as persistently seen only faults and flaws in the poor boys. The minister related many a touching incident in the lives of the departed, too, which illustrated their sweet, generous natures, and the people could easily see, now, how noble and beautiful those episodes were, and remembered with grief that at the time they occurred they had seemed rank rascalities, well deserving of the cowhide. The congregation became more and more moved, as the pathetic tale went on, till at last the whole company broke down and joined the weeping mourners in a chorus of anguished sobs, the preacher himself giving way to his feelings, and crying in the pulpit.
>
> There was a rustle in the gallery, which nobody noticed; a moment later the church door creaked; the minister raised his

streaming eyes above his handkerchief, and stood transfixed! First
one and then another pair of eyes followed the minister's, and then
almost with one impulse the congregation rose and stared while the
three dead boys came marching up the aisle, Tom in the lead, Joe
next, and Huck, a ruin of drooping rags, sneaking sheepishly in the
rear! They had been hid in the unused gallery listening to their own
funeral sermon!

Aunt Polly, Mary, and the Harpers threw themselves upon
their restored ones, smothered them with kisses and poured out
thanksgivings. . . .

Suddenly the minister shouted at the top of his voice: "Praise
God from whom all blessings flow—*sing*!—and put your hearts
in it!"

What a death! I, for one, would cheerfully sit through a few
weeks or months of "It feels like Mallory died" for a chance to
watch my hometown gather together to mourn my rare promise,
grieve over what were after all only the most minor of faults, rend
their garments in grief for not having praised me more often, only
to dazzle them by descending from the rafters and guide them
into amazement and song. What theatrically inclined transsexual
wouldn't jump at the chance?

And who could be so unreasonable as to not permit their loved
ones the opportunity to express sorrow or a sense of loss at the
prospect of change—in short, the thinking goes, why must those
theatrically inclined transsexuals insist on monitoring and super-
intending the feelings of others? *You* may have the right to transition (though what grounds in which that right may be established
is unclear—you may very well be getting away with something, let's
revisit our generosity later), but certainly *we* have the concomitant
right to name our own emotions and go into mourning. All change
entails at least some loss, if only the loss of a certain type of poten-

tial or expectation. Everyone has the right to mourn a loss. *You're taking _____ away from us, at least let us hold a funeral.* And yet other changes, other losses, even significant ones, are not counted as bereavements. The problem with the forced-bereavement that is sometimes thrust upon the transitioner is that there is no point at which the transitioner can rush up the aisle, call an end to the eulogy, and lead the congregation in song, praising God from whom all blessings flow, putting their whole hearts into it.

On the one hand, here is death: stagnant, permanent, immobilized, silent, unvarying, inactive, formless, characterless, shrinking, constrictive, irreversible. On the other hand, here is transition: active, forceful, adaptable, energetic, animated, expansive, full of possibility, capacious, comprehensive, vital, ambitious. Loss may be a part of the project of transition, but hardly the primary or initializing force. The question for the transitioner, then, is how to act in such a way that one is not mistaken by friends and family for Death itself; how to cope with being merely *noticed* rather than *seen*, how to prepare oneself to announce the end of a funeral only to be met with, "No, you're dead, or as good as. We'll stick with our corpse, thanks."

I was prepared for a degree of sadness and grief from my loved ones when I started to transition. I had often been sad about it myself, and considered that sadness part of a natural, intelligible response. In some ways it was correct to describe my transition as the beginning of an unprecedented kind of life; in some ways it was correct to describe my transition as an involuntary forgetting—I lost the ability to be a woman, sometimes by nearly imperceptible degree, sometimes in a great rush. Things I had known for years I suddenly forgot. I lost fluency, capability, drive, familiarity in the project of my womanhood, and I sometimes felt that it had been taken from me by some unknowable and external force. How could I possibly want, how could *I* possibly be responsible for, something I did not understand, something that bewildered and startled me? I had begun my transition unwittingly when I asked myself why, even in a life often characterized by happiness and purpose, I so often worked so hard not to ask myself what I felt or wanted in a given moment; once I began to think about things I had previously decided were impossible to think about, the very definition of the world *impossible* began to change.

Unremarkable, everyday things became wildly impossible; baffling, sometimes contradictory, profoundly daunting things became possible and shortly thereafter absolutely necessary. Nothing had been taken from me; I was not beset by external, capricious forces, not subject to the vicious whims of something outside myself; my sense of self was not under siege. I had never taken the compass of the things I did not want to want. I knew how to fantasize and how to deny my fantasies. I knew how to take my cues from other people who seemed satisfied with my part in the order of our relationship and I knew how to sustain myself with sufficient private, plausibly deniable escape valves that made it possible to go on without asking difficult questions. Those early days of transition, where I tested the waters while steadfastly refusing to admit I was doing anything differently, were of course characterized by a sense of loss; loss was the only way I could understand myself at first. But the loss was not only necessary, it was inevitable, and it cleared room for the possibility of something new, compelling, shared, productive, and profoundly good. Loss was present; death wasn't.

There is something willfully perverse about bereavement in the face of new life. My hope is not to squash or censor the complicated feelings of non-transitioning people, but to reconsider the direction of their sorrow. One might grieve and be prepared for something else, some new experience or sentiment to join one's grief, to mingle and ultimately sweeten it, add richness and support and texture. But to enter into mourning, to reenact the rituals of death, to borrow its vernacular, is to cut off understanding, curiosity, possibility, knowledge before they have a chance to flourish.

I sometimes think of the phrase "deadnaming" as a capitulation to the sometimes-fatal language other people use about our transitions—an attempt to reroute the language of death, if we can't clear it away entirely. It is, I suppose, a useful-enough shorthand for "This name is not part of the project of life." Death, and the threat of death, must be met somehow, and it may be that we cannot invent a new vocabulary overnight. But whenever I hear someone refer to death-as-transition or transition-as-death I think of Paul's second letter to the Corinthians on the subject of the resurrection:

> For we know that if our earthly house, this tent, is destroyed, we have a building from God, a house not made with hands, eternal in the heavens. For in this we groan, earnestly desiring to be clothed with our habitation which is from heaven, if indeed, having been clothed, we shall not be found naked. For we who are in this tent groan, being burdened, not because we want to be unclothed, but further clothed, that mortality may be swallowed up by life . . . old things have passed away; behold, all things have become new.

Here there are persons with multiple bodies that give way to one another—sometimes subject to corruption and destruction, sometimes ascending and taking on new power, new structure, new capabilities; sometimes clothed and sometimes naked, sometimes longing to be more naked than they already are; sometimes clothed and longing for further clothing; capable of change and regeneration that necessarily involve death but do not end with it—here death is a creative power in service to the greater force, the greater reality of life. Here life swallows up death, and everyone is invited to look at it, to see the evidence of the persistence of life with their own new eyes. Praise God from whom all blessings flow—*sing*—and put your hearts into it.

Nora Ephron's *I Feel Bad About My Neck*, Transmasculine Edition

I feel bad about my neck. All the time. If you saw my neck, you might feel bad about it, too, but you'd probably be too polite to let on, unless you are the kind of person who says things like "Welcome to womanhood" in a tone that actually means "Shut up" when a trans woman references her own experience with sexism, in which case you might let on after all. In that case, you might say something to me like, "Well, what do you expect?" or "You get what you paid for." And you'd be right, sort of, but it'd still be rude.

If I said something to you on the subject—something like "I absolutely cannot stand my testosterone-induced neck acne"— you'd likely respond by saying something nice, like, "You can barely notice it," or "Well, at least it's not on your *face*." You'd be lying, of course, but I forgive you just the same. I tell lies like that all the time, mostly to friends who tell me that they're not sure yet if top surgery is right for them, but would I recommend it if they were thinking about it, and if so should they consider free grafts or medically tattooed nipples, and how important was prioritizing sensation to me, and do I think they might qualify for peri or keyhole and what have I heard about Mosser and is it true that most surgeons want you to go on T first, and if so is the neck acne on T really that bad? My experience is that "I can barely notice it" is code for "If you think you're going to trap me into acknowledging how bad your neck acne is by asking me for suggestions on how to treat it, you're dead wrong." It's dangerous to engage with such subjects, and we all know it. Because if you said, "Yes, your formerly smooth neck has since bloomed into a map of angry red blotches," I might end up being one of those people you read about in the tabloids in court suing their endocrinologist. Furthermore, and this is the point, it would be All My Fault. I am particularly sensitive to the All My Fault aspect of things, since I have never forgiven one of my friends for seeing almost immediate results with Hibiclens.

Sometimes I go out to lunch with my boyfr— I got that far into the sentence and caught myself. I suppose I mean my transmasc friends. We are no longer boys and have not been boys for fifteen years, although you wouldn't know it to hear us refer to ourselves in the third person. Anyway, sometimes we go out to lunch and I look around the table and realize we're all wearing turtleneck sweaters, like the cluelessly handsome barista in a Coffee Shop AU. Sometimes instead we're all wearing scarves, like Johnny Weir in 2009. Sometimes we're all wearing hand-knitted mittens from our equally transmasculine boyfriends and look like an advertisement for "carefully calculated queer coziness." It's sort of funny, because we're not neurotic about identity, and whenever any of us exhibits a tendency to rename himself after a character from A Separate Peace, someone else gently sits on his chest until the urge passes. We all look good for our age and various hormone levels. Except for our necks.

Oh, the neck acne. According to my dermatologist, the neck starts to go at 220ng/dL of testosterone, and that's that. You can slather yourself in Dr. Jart correcting cream, order those little overnight acne patches from Sephora, you can hire a facialist to perform the most hygienic and regular of extractions, but short of a surgically implanted turtleneck, there's not a damn thing you can do about the neck. We try to tell ourselves that chaos is not the only governing force in our lives, but our necks are the truth.

My own experience with my neck began shortly after I turned thirty. I started taking hormones that shot me into a sort of second puberty, and while I'd had plenty of experience with the occasional spot on my nose during the original go-round, this was my first time dealing with zits below the jawline. If you learn nothing else from reading this essay, dear reader, learn this: Never start testosterone therapy without first taking as many pictures as possible of your neck. Because even if you honestly believe that your well-being is more important than vanity, even if you record your first "Six Days on T" video thrilled beyond your own imagining, grateful to be alive, full of blinding insight about what's important and what's not, even if you vow to be eternally joyful about being on the planet Earth and never to complain about anything ever again, I promise you that one day soon, sooner than you can imagine, you will look in the mirror and think, *Do they manufacture testosterone that leaves the neck out of it?*

Assuming, of course, that you do look in the mirror. That's another thing about being at a certain point in my own transition that I've noticed: I try as much as possible not to look in the mirror, preferring instead to toggle the "Male" filter on FaceApp and consider the results a binding promise of what I will look like two years from now. If I pass a mirror, I avert my eyes. If I must look into it, I begin by squinting, so that if something really bad is looking back at me, I am already halfway to closing my eyes to ward off the sight. And if the light is good (which I hope it's not) I often do what so many folks two years into testosterone replacement therapy do when stuck in front of a mirror: I place my fingers carefully over the acne and stare wistfully at the smooth skin in between. (Here's something else I've noticed, by the way: If you want to get really, really depressed about your neck, sit in the car, assuming you have access to one, and look at yourself in the rearview mirror. What is it about rearview mirrors? I have no idea why, but there are no worse mirrors where necks are concerned. It's one of the genuinely compelling mysteries of modern life, right up there with the unstudied connection between people with PCOS and trans men. Maybe it has something to do with control. In a selfie, you're holding the phone, and it knows it can't get away with so much as a mirror, which is farther away and harder to throw.)

But my neck. This is about my neck. And I know what you're thinking: Why not just decrease your dose? I'll tell you why not. I don't have the time to go back to crying eleven times a day. The fact is, it's all one big ball of wax. If you lose the neck acne, you run the risk of crying eleven times a day again, and I would rather cry three times a week and have neck acne. One of my biggest regrets— bigger even than my marriage to Carl Bernstein—is that I didn't spend my pre-transition years staring lovingly at my neck. It never crossed my mind to be grateful for it. It never crossed my mind that I would be nostalgic about a part of my body that I took completely for granted.

Of course, it's true that now that I'm older and transitioning, I'm wise and sage and mellow. And it's also true that I honestly do understand just what matters in life, which is slowly virilizing my body through the careful administration of a specific sex hormone. But guess what? It's *my* neck.

CHAPTER 17

Powerful T4T Energy in Steve Martin's *The Jerk*

Something my girlfriend and I talk about a lot is T4T energy—couples, usually fictional, mostly heterosexual, that somehow manage to emblematize a particular trans-on-trans dynamic. Seymour and Audrey from *Little Shop of Horrors*, Sally Solomon and her all-transmasc entourage on *3rd Rock from the Sun*, Elizabeth Taylor's marriages to Richard Burton (although not, of course, her marriage to Eddie Fisher); wearing a yellow baby-doll dress to your wedding after being condemned by the Vatican for "erotic vagrancy" is perhaps the pinnacle of T4T. Morticia and Gomez Addams are another obvious example. A family that can turn themselves into the most popular pinball game of all time certainly carries with it a particular transsexual resonance, and while most members of my generation are fond of the Raúl Juliá/Anjelica Huston movies in the same way we were all fond of the broadly light-Gothic vibe of the late eighties and early nineties (bracketed roughly by *Beetlejuice* on one end and *The Craft* on the other, with *Death Becomes Her* serving as the tentpole holding up the middle, and the live-action *Casper* serving as the air being let out of the tires), the Addams family is to trans people what *Showgirls* was to people who would go on to have careers in New York media.

I'd had no idea the Addamses originated as a series of *New Yorker* cartoons, having first encountered the 1960s TV show in reruns as a kid. Morticia was the first of the family to appear, because trans women are trailblazers and pioneers and the backbone of our community. Her transfeminine concordance feels obvious: she wears a lot of chokers, has excellent cheekbones, is a head or two taller than her adoring husband, is super into community gardening and constantly deadheading roses, and has a warm, comfortable relationship with her own affectations. Everyone with a lick of sense loves Morticia, but what *is* Gomez Addams, besides "an obviously transsexual man"? Everyone in the Addams family slides neatly into type: Morticia is a Vampirella/Elvira type, Lurch is a Frankenstein's monster, Grandmama is a witch in the chipper vein of June Foray, Wednesday is a Goth girl, Pugsley is alternately a baby serial killer and a mad scientist, Uncle Fester is Rotwang, but what of Gomez? In some of the early comics he looks a bit like Peter Lorre, but that's not much to go on.

And yet I think Gomez is the key to figuring out why the Addams family got a film revival and T-shirt deals while nobody today really cares about the Munsters. Yvonne De Carlo as Lily Munster had a similarly iconic beauty; Eddie Munster (Butch Patrick) a perfectly serviceable transmasculine look (all werewolves are transmasculine); Al Lewis as Grandpa has an immediately recognizable Bill Hader vibe, but Herman Munster (Fred Gwynne) falls flat on his face where Gomez Addams takes bat-like flight. That's not to say the patriarch is the most important element of the transsexual family model, but if you don't get the father right to begin with, he's going to drag everyone else down with him. Let's say the transsexual father has the most negative potential. Herman Munster is the patchwork result of a hundred different sitcom dads, all lovable buffoons, all empty temper tantrums, all puddin'-headed dreamers who have to be protected from the harshness of reality by enterprising wives; he's someone to affectionately tolerate and just as affectionately avoid.

Gomez Addams is the best father in the world: unrepentantly, sincerely crazy about his wife, a nimble knife thrower, an acrobat (like most trans men, he has a background in gymnastics and a taste for fussy, expensive-looking accessories), a talented business-man with a healthy dislike for work, a brilliant, anarchic lawyer who's never lost or won a case, in short, a man capable of maintaining balance both within and outside of the family home.

Charles Addams described him thusly:

> Husband to Morticia (if indeed they are married at all) . . . a crafty schemer, but also a jolly man . . . sometimes misguided . . . sentimental and often puckish—optimistic, he is in full enthusiasm for his dreadful plots . . . is sometimes seen in a rather formal dressing gown . . . the only one who smokes.

Resolutely cheerful, unrepentantly sentimental, unfortunately prone to Peter Pan syndrome, in a bafflingly nonspecific relationship with a tall, beautiful woman, deeply enthusiastic about terrible hobbies, a tendency toward overdressing, neglectful or at the least careless of his health—Gomez Addams could have walked out of a pamphlet on trans-specific medical care from Vancouver Coastal Health.

In the 1964 pilot episode of the TV show (which aired, I think, about a week before the pilot for *The Munsters*), the local truancy board tries to force the Addamses to send Wednesday and Pugsley to school. Morticia fobs the officer off onto Gomez with "You must speak to my husband, the law is his responsibility," but Gomez can't stand the idea of parting with the kids at all: "Why have children just to get rid of them? I'm opposed to the whole nonsense." Then he blows up a train. The pleasure of the Addams family fantasy, obviously, aside from "What if all your relatives had been as enthusiastic about your goth phase as you were?" is about having a mom and dad who are absolutely wild about each other, where every individual member has at least one creative passion and the time and energy to dedicate to it, while also receiving praise and constructive criticism on how to improve, eventually becoming so excellent as to influence the rest of society into adopting nuclear disarmament (this happens at the end of the pilot).

One gets the idea, watching Gomez, that he delights in getting to be a man, short and boisterous and nurturing and bursting with hope and pocket watches. He's especially delighted to be a man married to a woman, *particularly* when that woman is Morticia Addams. It's hard to get the same idea watching Herman Munster, or indeed lots of non-trans men both on and off the screen; maybe Herman is *willing* to be a man, or simply resigned to the idea. Possibly he merely considers it sufficient compensation for also being a monster of Frankenstein, but it doesn't seem to strike him with renewed absurd glee every morning when he gets to wake up and be one. One can imagine Herman Munster waking in a spirit of tolerance, at most willing to get out of bed and face another day as the head of a family. Whereas it's very easy to imagine Gomez's inner euphoria-driven monologue when he wakes up every morning: *Ah, how wonderful! Another stormy day! Ahahaha! Once again, I'm a short and stocky husband and father, with a wife as tall as God! What luck!* Why else would he spend a thousand dollars a month on cigars, or own so many bathrobes with exquisitely-designed lapels, or tend so carefully to such a thin mustache?

"How long has it been since we've waltzed?" Gomez asks Morticia in the 1991 movie.

"Oh, Gomez," she says, sighing dramatically. "*Hours.*"

While *liking your wife* might not be a uniquely T4T experience, the Addamses have a sort of shared vocational glee that's hardly common for opposite-sex couples on either the big or the little screen. But it's not always *short enthusiastic man* plus *tall elegant woman*, either; one of the strongest T4T pairings either Grace or I had ever seen took us rather by surprise, when we rewatched *The Jerk* a few weeks ago and watched Bernadette Peters fall in love with Steve Martin. I'd forgotten just how wonderfully *strange* Steve Martin's body was as a young man, how he'd been effectively doing old-man drag since his late twenties when his hair went gray, how fluid and twitchy his limbs were both at once, like the Scarecrow stumbling, stealthily graceful, through the first few beats of "If I Only Had a Brain." I know, in some sense, that his hair *went gray*, of course, but in another sense it's perfectly true that Steve Martin was born with a full head of hair, the same color as a fistful of silver dollars. There was a long stretch in the eighties and nineties where he'd alternate between playing beleaguered, straitlaced patriarchs (*Planes, Trains and Automobiles*; *Parenthood*; *Father of the Bride*) and total basket cases (a henpecked neurosurgeon, a jazz guitarist in love with a body-swapping ghoul, a desperate fire chief borrowing the body of a better-looking man).

All of the basket cases are absolutely chockablock with transmasculine energy, if only because disembodiment (*The Man with Two Brains*), supernatural body-swapping (*All of Me*) and non-supernatural body-swapping (*Roxanne*) are surprisingly frequent motifs; the scene everybody remembers from *Roxanne* is when Steve Martin, fake nose and all, runs through a list of creative insults about his appearance in order to humiliate the guy who has failed to satisfyingly harass him. He goes on to borrow his friend Chris's body in order to woo-by-proxy Daryl Hannah. Daryl (a girl with a boy's name who was best known at the time for playing a mermaid who renames herself and hides out in a human body in *Splash*) eliminates the middleman by telling Martin directly: "All these other men, Charlie, they've got flat, featureless faces. No character, no fire, no *nose*. Charlie, you have a big nose. You have a beautiful, great, big, flesh-and-bone *nose*."

There's a dance sequence at the end of *All of Me* between Steve Martin and Lily Tomlin to, of course, the song "All of Me," a song filled with such obvious transsexual imagery that it feels a little embarrassingly on the nose to even mention it ("Why not take all of me? . . . Take my lips, I want to lose them / Take my arms, I'll never use them"). By this point Lily Tomlin's character is now happily residing in the body of Victoria Tennant's character (younger, beautiful, glamorous, blonde) after the two of them have been variously body-swapped into a vase, Steve Martin, and a horse, and after panning out to a full-length mirror the camera swings back to show Tomlin dancing in Martin's arms in one last swap. It's uncertain whether this is meant to show us what *he* will see when he looks at her for the rest of their lives together—if all the world will see Victoria Tennant while he sees Lily Tomlin—but the possibility exists.

He spins her around about three times faster than the music and she tumbles over his feet, throws her head back, and laughs. They end up shimmying back to back, pointing wildly at the floor and the ceiling, then get right back to twirling, followed by a modified Charleston (more enthusiastic than correct on Tomlin's part, both enthusiastic *and* correct on Martin's). Eventually he picks her up and swings her around; they peck each other gently on the lips and keep twirling over and over the infinite black-and-white-tile pattern reflected in the mirror. It's either the pinnacle of heterosexuality or a beautiful moment of gay and lesbian solidarity, and I've never been able to figure out exactly which one it is. It ends in collapse as the two of them tumble into a heap together, a pretend-fall that turns into a real one. Or two pretend-falls, one of them less obviously staged than the other. In the last shot, they disintegrate beautifully and whole-heartedly in a hall of mirrors.

It's in *The Jerk* that Steve's T4T energy is at its absolute best, I think, as he and Bernadette Peters speak to each other in the most baffling voices imaginable. His Navin Johnson spends most of the movie hunched over in the shape of a question mark, usually from excitement, but looking for all the world like he's just been binding too long. Navin meets Peters's Marie after rescuing the boy she's babysitting from a runaway model train. Bernadette Peters sounds like a cross between a strict governess and Betty Boop to begin with, and she plays her natural coo up to the hilt for these scenes. I can never quite place what voice Martin's doing in *The Jerk*. It's like he's testing out every voice he's ever heard until he can land on one he likes. He pitches it high, then low, drawls it, drags it out, rushes through sentences like a breathless toddler, sometimes going through puberty in a single sentence. This is how he asks her out for the first time:

NAVIN: Do you have any boyfriends?
MARIE: Not really.
NAVIN: Are they crazy? If I was a fellow, I'd be around all the time.

Later, trying to cover for the fact that his own girlfriend is trying to bust up their date, Navin says, "Look, these hoodlums are dangerous. I think we oughta get out of here before she sees us. . . . I always call a gang 'she.' It's like when you call a boat 'she,' or a hurricane 'she.' Or a girl. You can call a girl 'she.' That's just one of the many things you can call a 'she.'" Marie, solemnly carrying a handful of decapitated daisies, nods skeptically but doesn't contradict him. There's a lovely little moment that comes when the two of them walk along the beach at night together, singing

"Tonight You Belong to Me" and falling in love with each other. Toward the end of the song she pulls out a trumpet and plays a virtuosic little solo. Navin's face is at first full of soft surprise and delight, then infinitely tender wistfulness, and he says, "You know, while you were playing that just now, I had the craziest fantasy that I could rise up and float right down the end of this coronet, right through here, through these valves, right along this tube, and right up against your lips."

In every scene Navin acts like a recent arrival to his own body. He never seems to get used to it, always moving his arms and legs like he's trying to keep up with his own marionettist, unfailingly one step behind the news of his own sex. He's shocked and delighted when his first girlfriend acquaints him with his own dick, which he calls his "special purpose," having assumed that's what his mother meant when she told him he'd find his "special purpose" someday. He even writes home to share the good news:

> My dear family, guess what? Today I found out what my special purpose is for.
>
> Gosh, what a great time I had. I wish my whole family could have been here with me. Maybe some other time as I intend to do this a lot.
>
> Every chance I get.
>
> > Your loving son,
> > Navin.

And what could be more transsexually resonant than having an unnecessarily specific conversation with your family about your dick and your sex life? Then comes an unexpectedly utopian response: Navin's family members are all thrilled for him.

I once tried to explain my approach to transition to a friend using *The Jerk*'s most well-known scene, when Navin, having lost everything in a lawsuit brought against him by Carl Reiner, announces he's leaving both Marie and their extravagant mansion to find people who believe in him. He starts to stumble out of the house unshaven and disheveled, wearing a worn-out bathrobe with his pants down around his ankles, declaring to anyone who will listen that he doesn't need "any of this—I don't need this stuff, and I don't need you." Then he grabs an ashtray and clarifies, "I don't need anything except *this*, and that's it, and that's the only thing I need, is this. I don't need *this* or *this*. Just this ashtray." Then he sees a paddle game: "And this paddle game. The ashtray and the paddle game and that's all I need," and so on with a remote control, a box of matches, a lamp, a chair, and a magazine, until he can barely shuffle along the street, weighed down as he is by household detritus. (The spell is finally broken when he gets to his dog, who growls at him, at which point he says, "Well, I don't need my dog, then.") Even if you haven't seen *The Jerk*, you've seen that scene, and it felt like the most immediately useful shorthand for transition: the frequent and immediate reversals, the increasingly emphatic avowals, the insistence that *this* was always the end, right here, trying to establish the absolute bare minimum, constantly leveraging the future against the present, patently insincere declarations of self-sufficiency, the pants around the ankles. "Just this haircut, and nothing else. Just this new haircut, and an entirely new wardrobe, and that's all. I don't need anything else. Just this new short haircut, and an all-new wardrobe, and a doctor's appointment I'm going to cancel and then reschedule nineteen times, but I don't need to tell anyone else about this or reconsider anything else. Just the haircut, the wardrobe, the on-and-off doctor's appointment I'll never go to, and these secret therapy sessions. That's all I need! I don't need to change my name or talk to my friends. Oh, I need *testosterone patches*, obviously. But just these!

Just this ninety-day supply of low-dose testosterone patches, and the haircuts, and all the formless sweaters, and confusing my doctor, and the secret therapy, and nothing else."

By the end of *The Jerk* Navin is restored to Marie, to his family, to financial solvency, the paddle game, and his dog; he has everything he needs and nothing he doesn't. But the moment I think of as representative of these two, of the mutual recognition and tentative delight of their T4T energy, comes when they're first reunited after a long separation a little more than halfway through the movie. It's neither their first separation nor their last reunion. Marie is working as a cosmetologist in a department store, displaying the effects of a new face mask called Mascoderm on an elderly man named Irving as his wife and a number of other women watch. She promises that when they peel it off, his skin will be tighter, firmer, and look like someone else's skin entirely. "You'll be amazed. Get ready, Irving!" While they wait for the Mascoderm to do the work, she helps his wife pick out eyeshadow and lip tint for Irving post-transformation. "Let's try *everything*," his wife says, unwilling to foreclose on any possibilities, open to any and all imaginable futures. Meanwhile, Navin has snuck into the room, eager to surprise Marie, and switches places with Irving, settling in under the mask.

Marie bends over him and starts to peel off the Mascoderm. Irving's wife bites her nails. The crowd gasps. "Jeez," Marie says. "This shit really *works*." The two fall into each other's arms.

"What are you doing to my husband?" Irving's wife says, horrified. "Irving, are you *crazy*?" She pauses a moment, unsure of how to take this in, how to read what she's seeing. Then she starts hitting them both with her handbag, but Navin and Marie just keep kissing. Rising up and floating right down to the end of this coronet, right through here, through these valves, right along this tube, and right up against each other's lips.

Did You Know That Athena Used to Be a Tomboy?

ATHENA: *You know, when I sprang out of my father's head fully formed and kitted out in battle armor head-to-toe, if I'm honest, I was doing it for his attention, too—for male approval. What I'm saying is, I get it. I didn't want to be a girl, either, but then I learned to love myself, and to become the tutelary of Athens. Have you tried being the tutelary of Athens?*

DEUTERAGONIST: I just don't want you doing anything extreme. It's not that I don't understand where you're coming from. God, no! It's not that I'm not sympathetic. We've all been there. Currer Bell, and so on. Slick my hair back, spit on the subway, and demand a raise. But you have to know where to stop with this sort of thing. But I get it! Your heart's in the right place, and you've got a good head on your shoulders, so most of your body is in correct working order.

CHORUS: Look, we hate to see you go. Hate to lose a valuable member of the team. But we understand—all good things must come to an end—but could you do us a favor? Could you just talk for a few minutes about what you think we could have done to keep you as a customer? Anything we should bear in mind for the future, anything that might have encouraged you to renew your contract? Are you sure you don't want to change your mind? We hate to see you go. You know, we all used to be tomboys, so we get where you're coming from. You know you don't have to take it all the way. Look at Athena! Sprang completely grown from her father's head—probably had eight or nine older brothers who taught her how to work on cars—bypassed her mother entirely; born in full battle armor—and look at her now. Tutelary of Athens! Goddess of owls, and so on. You can be the tutelary of Athens and still be a woman. Have you tried being the tutelary of Athens? Have you tried everything?

ATHENA: *You know, if I were to spring out of my father's head fully formed and kitted out in battle armor head-to-toe nowadays, they'd probably diagnose me with dysphoria, too, and have me signed up for dick-installation surgery before dinnertime. And I really don't think it's fair to sign someone up for dick-installation surgery before they even get the chance to become the tutelary of Athens.*

CHORUS: Well, of course we'd all be trans *now*, wouldn't we? Anyone born nowadays, that's just a given, they just—someone tells you at school, or something—everyone's trans now. Not like when we were kids, when people still understood when someone was being metaphorical. We're all a *little* bit that way, so I don't know why you have to take it so seriously. It's a little embarrassing. Did someone put you up to this?

You can tell us. If you want to just climb a tree, climb a tree!

DEUTERAGONIST: I used to think I was a boy all the time, when I was a girl. Thinking you're a boy is a big part of being a girl. We all thought we were boys, but thank God no one took us seriously. It's time to take girls seriously about not taking girls who are boys seriously. When I was a girl, I thought of boyish things, but when that which is complete has come, then that which is in part will be done away. When I was a girl, I spoke as a boy, I understood as a boy, I thought as a boy; but when I became a woman I put away boyish things. For now we see in a mirror, dimly, but soon we shall see face to face. *Welcome to being a woman.* Now I know in part, but then I shall know just as I also am known.

ATHENA: *What about all the little Athenas who are springing forth from their father's heads as full-grown adults in head-to-toe armor? What kind of a message is this sending them, about what it means to spring forth from their father's heads as full-grown adults in head-to-toe armor while also being women? There are lots of different kinds of women, some of whom spring forth fully formed from their father's heads in battle regalia, fully forth and fully formed and fully sprung and full-fathered, full-figured and fully women, and what kind of message are they picking up? Not to mention Artemis. What kind of message is this sending to vulnerable, virginal goddesses of the hunt?*

DEUTERAGONIST: I mean, if I were thirty years younger— if I were twenty-five years younger—if I were eighteen years younger—God, if I were just ten years younger—if I were a year and a day younger—if I were a month younger—if you'd asked me just five minutes ago, four and a half even, if I'd picked up on the first ring instead of the third, I'd transition. Hell, I'd transition. Oh my God, I wish I could transition. Ask me again, but sooner. Come back yesterday. Come back a week ago. What good are you to me now, when I am —this? Where were you when there was still summer in my heart? Come back a month ago, a decade, but come back to before I had to forgive you. Just come back and ask again; I'll wait if it takes forever this time.

CHORUS: She was *such* a pretty girl. Shame.

ATHENA: *Oh, I don't know. Let's not get carried away—she wasn't that pretty.*

CHORUS: Pretty enough, then. Still a shame, though.

ATHENA: *Oh, yes, still a shame, that.*

CHAPTER 18

It's Hard to Feel Sad Reading Hans Christian Andersen Because It's Just Another Story About a Bummed-Out Candlestick That Loves a Broom and Dies

When I was twelve my father and I went to Boston Market every week to discuss the work of Søren Kierkegaard (my father's idea) and to eat as much roast chicken skin as possible without exciting commentary (mine). My general impression of Denmark at the time was that it had produced two deeply unhappy redheaded men, Kierkegaard and Hans Christian Andersen, who invented fairy tales, broken engagements, and being gay and religious at the same time. I found them both deeply compelling, although it was clear to me from a much tenderer age which of those weeping Danes had the lion's share of my attention and affection.

I was interested enough in learning about Søren Kierkegaard, and particularly interested in watching what Søren Kierkegaard did to my father's face as he discussed it. He became animated, choked-up, organized, earnest, charismatically tapped into a long legacy of persuasive male sadness. My father was a very disciplined eater, and his order was always the same: one-quarter chicken (all white meat, no gravy), steamed broccoli, green beans, no to the complimentary corn bread. If the cashier nonetheless absent-mindedly placed a piece in his order, he would section off a tidy two-bite-sized chunk and set it aside to act as dessert, throwing the rest away, though I was always happy to finish whatever corn bread remained. My father always made a show of restraining his appetites but never his sentiment.

The first story Hans Christian Andersen ever published was about a candle that did not feel appreciated, which is in some ways representative of his life's output. Women, generally speaking, didn't want to marry him; men, generally speaking, didn't want to exchange love letters with him. Charles Dickens found him an unwelcome houseguest and said so to anyone who would listen. Even Kierkegaard thought him a chump: "He sits and cries over his unhappy heroes, who are doomed to perish, and why? Because Andersen is the man he is. The same joyless fight that Andersen himself has fought in life is now repeated in his poetry." I myself often felt deep resentment upon finishing one of his stories, as if he had written them with the studied intention of spoiling my fun: *I have to carry the weight of the personal tragedies of candlesticks around with me now?* But he wasn't wrong, Hans, and of all the miserable chumps in the world, his was the most joyful chumpery. Yes, every object in one's home, from silverware to shoes, was imbued with longing and frustration, but there was always transformation and death to look forward to, an abrupt and massive metamorphosis with a built-in heavenly audience. And sometimes the stories ended in big, showy weddings instead of death (or both, which was the best kind).

I was already half convinced in the way many children are that the objects in my room were alive in the way people were alive, capable of receiving and transmitting spiritual impressions of experiences like rejection or insult. This was especially true in matters of seniority. I knew *Toy Story* to be a lie when I saw it at age nine because it tried to tell me that my toys were persons in the same way I was a person, that they simply waited for me to leave the room before playing out their copy-versions of my life. I knew their aliveness was nothing like mine. Outside the suburban-casual rules of the Midwest held among my peers, my bedroom was a Hapsburg court. As the primary *player* with the toys I was responsible for soothing hurt feelings, paying tribute to age and rank, stifling social rivalries and dampening feuds, not a sovereign but their highest-ranking servant. Their souls were slower and older than mine, their relationship to language significantly streamlined. They were either *pleased* or *displeased* with the order in which I took them out and played with them, their nightly resting places on my bed or in the closet; I was either acting in accordance with their wishes or in defiance of them. Whatever games I was playing with them throughout the day, whatever adventures I took them on, there was always the *shadow game* underneath of making sure they were all satisfied with how they were being handled. Hardly a night went by that I knew I had not shorted one of them, that at least one of my dearest companions had been tucked into bed with a grievance against me, that I would wake up in the morning already at a social deficit.

Hans Christian Andersen knew this. Søren Kierkegaard may have asked me to consider the anxiety of Abraham, the anxiety of readiness, of "Here I am," of the possibility of murder and an uncertain number of sons—to prepare to deal with God. But Hans prepared me to *be* a god. Everything around you is alive and bursting with unrequited love and it's your fault, or at least your responsibility—what are you prepared to do about it?

THAT MIGHT MAKE FOR SOME HIGH-INTENSITY FAIRY TALES, BUT HE SOUNDS LIKE AN EXHAUSTING HOUSEGUEST

It's easy to imagine why Dickens found him an unpleasant room-mate. One can picture him tiptoeing down the hallway at two in the morning, whispering "Are you awake?" (in the tone of someone who knows perfectly well that you *aren't* awake, they're just afraid to commit to saying, *Wake up, I want to talk to you*) because he wants to know if you think pine trees ever get lonely.

"I'm sure pine trees have lots of other pine tree friends," you-as-Dickens might suggest in the hopes of returning to sleep.

"Yes, but what if *this one* didn't? What if all the other pine trees were cruelly indifferent to him, and then he was chopped down and made into firewood, or the cross that Christ was murdered on?"

To which you might respond that the Romans didn't make crosses out of pine trees, hoping the conversation might end there.

"What if a serving ladle fell in love with snuffbox, but they could never touch?"

To which you would have no proper answer.

The premise of so many Andersen stories fits in neatly with the kinds of questions very young children ask: *What if a tin soldier fell in love with a music box and then they both caught on fire? What if a flower fell in love with a bee that died of thirst? What if a girl stepped on some bread and turned into a bird that flew directly into the sun? What if a needle wanted to die but couldn't? What if your skin hurt so bad that no matter how carefully you were wrapped up, no matter how tenderly you were put to bed, nothing helped? What, then?*

I can think of myself, twelve, at a midwestern Boston Market, eating discarded chicken skin, and picture either a remarkably

messy young girl or a strangely fussy young boy trying to follow
along to *Fear and Trembling*. Nothing was quite fixed at that point.
But at thirty the great question of my life became *What if you were
a man, sort of?* Never mind what "sort of," "were," or "man" meant
in that moment—the question itself felt to me ridiculous, intru-
sive, unhelpful, a joke carried too far, a distant acquaintance living
in Scandinavia taking "Well, look me up if you're ever in town" as an
excuse to move in with me and my family for five weeks and throw
fits on the lawn. Hans tried to warn me that the world was full of
too much feeling, not too little, and that I was going to have to pay
attention to it.

THERE'S A LITTLE TOWN OUTSIDE OF SANTA BARBARA THAT COSPLAYS AS A TRADITIONAL DANISH VILLAGE WITH A HANS CHRISTIAN ANDERSEN MUSEUM

- I'VE NEVER BEEN INSIDE THE DANISH VILLAGE MYSELF BECAUSE THAT TOWN IS TRANSPHOBIC AS ALL GET-OUT (OR STAY-IN)
- LAST YEAR I STOPPED THERE FOR GAS AND I GOT HUSTLED OUT OF A PUBLIC RESTROOM AND MY GIRLFRIEND GOT YELLED AT IN A BAKERY
- IF YOU'RE IN THE NEIGHBORHOOD COULD YOU LET ME KNOW IF THE LOCAL MUSEUM OF DANISH-AMERICAN HISTORY IS ANY GOOD AND ALSO PICK ME UP A WIENERBRØD OR SOMETHING
- I DON'T THINK THERE'S ANYTHING INSIDE THAT MUSEUM THAT COULD TEACH ME SOMETHING ABOUT HANS CHRISTIAN ANDERSEN I DON'T ALREADY KNOW
- I FELT ABSOLUTELY TERRIBLE OUTSIDE OF THAT RESTROOM AND I FEEL TERRIBLE THINKING ABOUT IT NOW

NOT FREEZING TO DEATH IS HARDER THAN IT LOOKS

I don't mean to suggest that Hans Christian Andersen knew I was trans before I did; I'm not sure it's strictly correct to say that I was trans before *I* knew I was. But I knew in that Boston Market, and in my childhood bedroom, and my whole life long, that Hans Christian Andersen knew *something* about me that Søren Kierkegaard didn't, and that whatever he knew was going to be tricky— was already tricky. *The Little Match-Girl* works in the same way:

- This little girl is going to freeze to death!
- This little girl is going to freeze to death!
- This little girl is beginning to freeze to death!
- This little girl is going to freeze to death!
- This little girl has frozen to death!

That was the greatest appeal Hans Christian Andersen (and most nineteenth-century child-adjacent literature, really) had for me: how often and in how many different ways he could ask the question "What if you were extremely beautiful and then you died, and dying made you even more beautiful, and then a lot of sympathetic people watched you dying and said things like, 'Oh, how terrible that someone so beautiful is dying, how awful'?" My appetite at six, at nine, at twelve, at thirty, for stories like that were as boundless as my appetite for roast chicken skin; any fantasy that involved doing nothing when faced with important decisions while being praised for my appearance appealed to me. But one must, if one does not spontaneously die, do *something* when faced with important decisions.

In 2011, the Presbyterian Church USA (PCUSA) approved Amendment 10-A, which relaxed the rules against gay parishioners seeking church office, allowing each member-church discretion in deciding whether to ordain them. Both the San Francisco and San

Jose Presbyteries voted "yes" on the amendment. Three years later, my parents' church voted to leave the denomination, officially citing "ease of operating multi-site churches," and joined a relatively new denomination known as A Covenant Order of Evangelical Presbyterians, whose Essentials of the Reformed Tradition declares "We therefore hold one another accountable to . . . maintain chastity in thought and deed, being faithful within the covenant of marriage between a man and a woman as established by God at the creation or embracing a celibate life as established by Jesus in the new covenant." The church paid PCUSA over $8 million in order to buy back the titles to its own property; no one in the church leadership ever cited gay marriage or ordination as a reason for the move, and I was very careful never to ask. I wanted very badly for it simply to have been bad timing.

In "The Tinder-Box," a frightful-looking witch advises a soldier on where to find a great treasure:

> "On entering the first of the chambers, you will see a large chest, standing in the middle of the floor, and upon it a dog seated, with a pair of eyes as large as teacups. But you need not be at all afraid of him; I will give you my blue checked apron, which you must spread upon the floor, and then boldly seize hold of the dog, and place him upon it. If you would rather have silver money, you must go into the second chamber. Here you will find another dog, with eyes as big as mill-wheels; but do not let that trouble you. Place him upon my apron, and then take what money you please. If, however, you like gold best, enter the third chamber, where there is another chest full of it. The dog who sits on this chest is very dreadful; his eyes are as big as a tower, but do not mind him."

I used to have the *hardest* time remembering the difference between bathos and pathos (a rapid-fire shift from something meaningful to something banal and an attempt to arouse sympathy or sentiment, roughly and in that order). I might have had it explained patiently and clearly to me one hundred times, but I could still never get much further than "pathos with a 'B' on it," especially because *some* of the time, apparently, bathos really is just short for "a surfeit of pathos." In a pinch I could remember that Alexander Pope invented it, but when it came to retaining any further information on the subject, my brain was like a wet, angry dog in a bucket.

I spent countless nights anguishing over whether or not to get top surgery, about whether I'd be willing to carry bright red scars right on the front of my body for the rest of my life in order to have the chest I wanted. A few months after my surgery, someone on Twitter offhandedly mentioned that they look like two Twizzlers. They were exactly right—that's *just* what they looked like. And I knew in that moment that I really always had known what bathos was, that it was terribly simple, but that I'd always been so afraid of finding out I was too stupid to understand.

The dog who sits on this chest is very dreadful; his eyes are as big as a tower, but do not mind him. I've got an apron that defeats him.

Dirtbag Sappho

A HYMN TO APHRODITE

Look, Aphrodite, man. Look. You know who your father is,
and you've got hobbies, which puts you two up on me.
Yes? Yes. So going out of your way
to break my spirit with adversity,
given our respective circumstances,
seems heavy-handed for a goddess known for subtlety.
Come on, man. Just: Come on.
Leave your father's gorgeous house,
take your father's stylish car (if ever before
you took a single one of my calls without
screening it, take this one, please)
come down in wings and darkness
and *get here in time*. Smile,
if you can find the energy,
or the time to wipe one over your deathless mouth.
(It's one thing to tell a god to smile but where I can't command
            I will ask:
with all that you've got to smile about, why refuse?)
But go ahead and ask me: What's

the matter now, Sappho, why
this round of calls, what's the new
pain lodged in my ghoulish heart?
Fine, fine, "What's her name *this* time, girl-chick,
whose kiosk in the mall did you hang around at for too long
after her shift got over, before her ride got there?
I'll have her car
idling in your driveway
before she has time to pray to other gods."
A dick move, if you ask me,
bragging like that.
Look, just get here, okay? Because (1) I gave you
my only set of spare keys years ago, (2) you know
I'd do the same for you if you needed anything,
so just fulfill what needs fulfilling and don't
drag out my emptiness
(3)
just be a fucking friend, like you said
you'd be. Okay?

FRAGMENT 31

Oh, fuck, man, fuck me, fuck fuck.—
Some guys get to sit across the room from *you*
and listen to the sound your mouth makes
(jesus don't *say* things like that),
I just mean: you laugh sometimes, and it sends
my heart on worldwide tour. It's all chest cavity panic.
I mean the minute I catch eyes of you there's no
thought left in me,
gag me, fuck me *up*—: look, I'll confirm all this
low-grade fever, this skin-ruining crush is pure damage

Status: Knees week, mom's spaghetti—
you know the rest,
and I'm bitch-sweating *yikes*, and the shakes
are coming on quick, no letting up, it's all over
for me, I'm fourteen seconds south of dying,
I'm *fully* offline;
but this piece-of-shit me isn't going anywhere, Hiiiiii—

FRAGMENT 145
IMPORTANT ROCKS DO NOT MOVE

FRAGMENT 156
I like her purse.
It's well-ordered and free of sand,
and she's not stingy with a spray of perfume,
but that girl's dumb as hell.

FRAGMENT 22
She wore a full-on dress once. Oh my God,
you remember the eclipse on Cyprus?
It was like that. A national event.
That dress was an emergency.

FRAGMENT 90
It's no good, I quit,
Mother or whomever else is concerned, I
officially resign from
weaving, and all other work.
        You can
blame God, if you want,
just let me lie here on the tile

God sent me an assassin
the day he showed me
that boy's face. Have you seen it?
Who can *weave*, at a time like this?

SAPPHO AT 16

Everybody says their girlfriend is hot.
Armies of girlfriends, some on horses, some not,
bobbing just outside of port on the Girlfriend Ships,
Whatever; everyone has to say it, but they can't all be right.

Take Helen (please!), whom "all Greece hates"
     hot like burning, and so *knows* from fine,
     what did it take to get her to leave,
     a top-ten husband (universally agreed-upon
as one of the best, even from people who normally
can't grind out one nice thing to say about a man),

     shut up her house,
     throw her kid out the window,
     turn her parents out in the streets
     (which, incidentally, any one of us would do
at the prospect of a thorough dicking at the hands
of a face like that. If faces can be said to have hands, which
they can't)

     That sort of dick-longing is *adaptable*,
maneuverable,
     and *aerodynamic*. It reminds me
of the last girl I dated.

How to put this? I've seen my girl's face and your man's.
I'd sooner watch the turn of her steps
or the side of her face than your whole boyfriend,
who on his best day looks like Kashi cereal.

CHAPTER 19

Dante Runs into
Beatrice in Paradise

When I was fourteen I had the following items temporarily con-fiscated at a Christian extreme sports summer camp: *Time* magazine, *Seventeen* magazine, and Dante's *Inferno* and *Purgatorio*. (I don't remember much about the extreme sports; I know it was billed as a sort of zip-lining, belaying, rock-scrambling center, but mostly I just played tennis and politely avoided signing a virginity pledge.) I don't suppose I really believed I would have time to read all of them in a four-week session, but I wanted very much to be *seen* reading them by my fellow Christian extreme sports campers. Instead the Dante books were whisked away to the infirmary and bound together with masking tape that I had to gingerly peel off myself at the end of summer.

I spent the rest of the summer after camp making my way through the *Purgatorio* and sorting through everything I'd heard at camp. The difference between a broadly centrist evangelical home environment in suburban Chicago and fundamentalist-flexible evangelical summer camp in rural Missouri is significant; this had been my first real encounter with young-earth creation-ism and Christian complementarianism, and I'd come away puzzled and contemplative. A very earnest Bible teacher with a Ned Flanders mustache had drawn a diagram of the antediluvian earth to explain how an atmospheric canopy might have enabled Methuselah to reach 969 years and that the likeliest inspiration for my desire to become a pastor someday was the devil seeking to overturn male headship. He was also very kind to me. It seemed fairly reasonable that he was incorrect both about the canopy and the nature of female leadership, but his authority seemed both plausible and well-intended, so I dutifully turned the possibilities over in my mind for a few weeks before deciding against them.

One gets the sense, in both the *Inferno* and the *Purgatorio*, that Dante wishes very badly to include his guide Virgil among the ranks of the blessed rather than in Limbo, where the shades of great spirits are "only so far punished that without hope we live on in desire." The air there is alive with the sound of constant, eternal sighing, and Dante's heart is "seized in great grief" to think of all the worthy souls who dwell there (*Inf. Canto IV*). At the end of *Purgatorio*, Virgil is quietly swapped out for Beatrice in the Earthly Paradise, after leading Dante through the final wall of fire at the end of the Terrace of Lust, where the soon-to-be-redeemed transmit quick, careful greetings like ants tapping antennae together to avoid the kind of lingering touch that dawdles into sin. The lustful are divided into two groups that hustle swiftly around the terrace, each calling out homo- and heterosexual examples of carnality like rival sports fans: "Sodom and Gomorrah!" "Pasiphaë!"

Th' escorting spirits turn'd with gentle looks
Toward me, and the Mantuan spake: "My son,

Here torment thou mayst feel, but canst not death.

Remember thee, remember thee, if I

Safe e'en on Geryon brought thee: now I come

More near to God, wilt thou not trust me now?

Of this be sure: though in its womb that flame

A thousand years contain'd thee, from thy head

No hair should perish. If thou doubt my truth,

Approach, and with thy hands thy vesture's hem

Stretch forth, and for thyself confirm belief.

Lay now all fear, O lay all fear aside.

Turn hither, and come onward undismay'd."

I still, though conscience urg'd' no step advanc'd.

When still he saw me fix'd and obstinate,

Somewhat disturb'd he cried: "Mark now, my son,

From Beatrice thou art by this wall

Divided." As at Thisbe's name the eye

Of Pyramus was open'd (when life ebb'd

Fast from his veins), and took one parting glance,

While vermeil dyed the mulberry; thus I turn'd

To my sage guide, relenting, when I heard

The name, that springs forever in my breast.

He shook his forehead; and, "How long," he said,

"Linger we now?" then smil'd, as one would smile

Upon a child, that eyes the fruit and yields.

Into the fire before me then he walk'd;

And Statius, who erewhile no little space

Had parted us, he pray'd to come behind.

I would have cast me into molten glass

To cool me, when I enter'd; so intense

Rag'd the conflagrant mass. The sire belov'd,
To comfort me, as he proceeded, still
Of Beatrice talk'd. "Her eyes," saith he,
"E'en now I seem to view." From the other side
A voice, that sang, did guide us, and the voice
Following, with heedful ear, we issued forth,
There where the path led upward.

                               —*Inferno Canto XXVII*

Another river, another pair of guide and guided, another traveler convinced his journey is ending in destruction just before emerging safely on the other side. Virgil, unlike Hopeful, can stir no higher than the Earthly Paradise, and cannot comment on matters celestial; Dante must exchange a man he has never met for a woman he saw twice before she died. They pass together through the fire, and Virgil offers Dante both "crown and mitre, sovereign o'er thyself." At the top of Mount Purgatory Dante is dazzled by a succession of women—Leah, Rachel, Matilda, the seven heavenly Virtues, Jerome's elders, the epistles and a griffin—and finally Beatrice, heading the processional. The sight of the woman he loves sweeping grandly down the aisle sends Dante into a panic: He has climbed out of Hell, scaled Purgatory, knocks on the gate of Heaven only to come down with *cold feet*. It's at this point that he turns to Virgil for, oddly, maternal comfort: "towards Virgil I turn'd me to leftward, panting, like a babe/That flees for refuge to his mother's breast." But there is no Virgil to offer comfort nor even say goodbye to:

But Virgil had bereav'd us of himself,
Virgil, my best-lov'd father; Virgil, he
To whom I gave me up for safety: nor,

All, our prime mother lost, avail'd to save
My undew'd cheeks from blur of soiling tears.

"Dante, weep not, that Virgil leaves thee: nay,
Weep thou not yet: behooves thee feel the edge
Of other sword, and thou shalt weep for that."

—*Inferno Canto XXX*

Don't cry for *him*—*I'll* give you something to cry about. To put it another way: Do not cry when you lose the things you love that kept you from God, *cry over the things you love that keep you from God.* The man with the Ned Flanders mustache was wrong about me, but not because I was not a woman. (For that matter, I'm not a pastor, either.) To say *As a woman, approach God thusly* or *As a man, do not approach God in such-and-such a manner, but in thus-and-so a manner* is to put the cart before the horse. Dante approaches Paradise "return'd from the most holy wave, regenerate / If 'en as new plants renew'd with foliage new/Pure and made apt for mounting to the stars," purged of sinful memories by the river Lethe and restored to memories of virtue by the river Eunoe.

In *The Music Man*, the mayor's wife, Eulalie, teaches dance to the leading ladies of the town and can periodically be heard in the background instructing them in a voice that is somehow both unusually deep and delivered in falsetto: "Lovely, ladies, lovely and turn. Take the body with you!" I found that line unutterably hilarious, and often repeat it to myself whenever I'm in a rush to get out the door: "Taaaaake the body with you." If ultimately the goal is "neither to marry nor be given in marriage, like the angels" (Matt. 22:30), then it may be that the body, and the rules governing the body, and the standards and strictures appertaining to the body, must needs be checked at the gate between the earthly and the celestial, but *something* must be resurrected, and until then, you've got to take the body with you. It may be, after all, that the body is only confiscated and bound with masking tape before being returned from the infirmary, and if you can't undo the marks left on the cover it's still legible once you open to the front page.

How I Intend to Comport Myself
When I Have Abs Someday

When I have abs someday, no one will ever know about it, just a little secret between me and my torso. Unless they find out by accident, like if I happen to be reaching for something above my head in front of a couple of people—maybe I'm reaching for a jar of lentils for a dear friend who can't reach it but I can, because they're five foot five and I'm five foot seven and three-quarters inches tall, and I'm the sort of friend who will happily grab a jar of lentils for a dear friend as we prepare a wholesome, simple meal together—and my shirt rides up, and accidentally now a couple of (just a couple, not all of them, I have lots of friends) my casual friends (not my closest friends) see that I have abs, and it's sort of a moment—not a big one, but definitely a few of them say under their breath, "Did you know that he even had abs?" and "I never would have guessed that he had abs, because he's so engrossed in his work and really laid-back about body stuff" and "Wow, abs," and then I'd have gotten whatever I was reaching for (lentils, or another equally filling pulse or legume), and the moment would sort of pass without remark. Probably no one would say anything out loud, because it would be obvious to them I don't make a big deal out of having abs, so nobody wants to be the one to make a big deal out of it.

But they'll talk about it among themselves, like maybe when I leave the room to go to the bathroom or, more likely, to check on some bread that I decided to bake last-minute for our wholesome, simple, lentil-based meal, because I make bread often enough that I have a pretty quick recipe memorized (I'm not fussy about bread making, it's really pretty intuitive for me at this point) and they might even text a friend or two to say, "Did you know that he had abs?"

"I had no idea!" that friend or two might respond. "But you know, now that you mention it, I can totally see it."

And that'll be the end of the conversation, probably, because they respect my privacy, but it'll certainly add a new dimension to what my friends think of me, and they'll be particularly struck by the realization because usually when people get abs you hear about it right away. Just not with me, because having abs doesn't define me as a person, even though I have abs now.

"Do you think he . . . *knows* that he has abs?"

"Oh, don't be ridiculous. Of course he knows!!!" But they'll wonder. Maybe I haven't noticed!!! I don't *dress* like I know that I have abs, which isn't to say that I'm a sloppy dresser, just that I don't dress in a very show-offy way. I don't dress in a studiously non–show-offy way, either, of course—I'm not one of those guys with abs who goes out of his way to really drive the point home that he doesn't have to put effort into his appearance. It's kind of hard to describe, actually, but basically I just manage to fall into this sweet spot, sartorially speaking, where I'm neither trying too hard nor trying too hard to *look* like I'm not trying too hard. Which is a really nice change of pace for a guy with abs.

When I have abs someday, the photo roll on my phone will be mostly full of sunsets and interesting-looking floral arrangements put together by some designers I know, maybe with a few shots of some of (not all, I have lots) my friends in candid moments. I'll also call my grandmother a lot, and cut out recipes I think she'll like from the newspaper and mail them to her, because I keep a few rolls of Forever stamps and a stack of envelopes in my odds-and-ends drawer so I'm always ready to send her something. My living arrangement is kind of characterized by casual anticipation of my own needs and the needs of others, which means that things tend to run pretty smoothly with minimal effort—kind of like my abs.

The other great thing I'll do when I have abs someday is have the kind of relationship to food that pretty much everyone universally agrees is relaxed, healthy, correct, and makes me a lot of fun to be around at mealtime. Whenever someone spontaneously suggests going to IHOP after a wonderful, electric evening of surprising connections that's fostered the beginning of several new and unlikely friendships, I'll always offer to drive. Not because I *need* to be the one who drives. I never get weird when someone else drives, I'm just ready to drive because I own my own car and always remember to renew my license on time. When we get there, to IHOP or some rough equivalent, because I'm equally comfortable at chain restaurants that remind me of all my less-than-genteel Midwestern roots as well as upscale diners with, like, fresh lemon-ricotta variations, I'll eat whatever number of pancakes is neither ostentatiously over-the-top nor pointedly less than what everyone else is eating. I'll just really enjoy whatever number of pancakes sounds good to me, and I'll stop eating when I'm full. My relationship to pancakes isn't punitive, doesn't require denial or the language of guilt, and is never followed up by a trip to the gym; food is something more than fuel but something less than an obsession with me. I don't have a compulsive need to finish whatever's in front of me. (Not that I'm a food waster!) It'll be such a relief, just being around me as I eat a meal, like a temporary reprieve from the politics of food and the internal pressure to be constantly body-positive.

I'll also cover the whole bill!!! Not in a way that suggests I'm trying to avoid the slow and challenging work of establishing meaningful intimacy over time, nor in a way that sets off any alarm bells about neurotic spending, and definitely not in a way that makes it seem like I'm trying to establish any kind of relational superiority with money. "It's just pancakes," I'll say. "It's twenty dollars for the whole bill, it's not a big deal!!! It's just a bunch of warm bread, I'm only doing this because it's the cheapest way to treat!!! Relax, I've got it!!! Don't you *dare* try to pay me back! Fine, buy me a coffee the next time we see each other, if it's so important to you," because while I'll definitely be generous I'll have no interest in establishing dominance through check-grabbing, so I'll be equally comfortable being treated as I am treating others.

When I have abs someday, I'll still have plenty of time to dedicate to my work, because I'm incapable of being distracted by my own abs. I *value* them but they're not my highest priority. "His art seems better, somehow," people will say. "Since he got abs, I mean. I don't really know how to explain it, because he definitely hasn't changed as a result of getting abs. Making abs? Having abs? He hasn't changed at all because of his abs, but at the same time it's undeniably true that his art is both intangibly but demonstrably suppler these days, and it all happened around the same time. He's the same but also better."

"Art?" someone else might ask. "I thought he was a writer."

"Oh, it's *all* art," people will respond. "His writing is definitely art now, if it wasn't art before. He's an artist, definitely. And obviously it's not that the abs have improved his art, because if he stopped having abs tomorrow I know it would still be just as good. The abs have had both no effect on him and also elevated the excellent things about him that were already there, simultaneously."

When I have abs someday, even though I'll barely notice my own abs, I certainly won't irritate people by performatively not

noticing my own abs. I'll have so thoroughly and casually con-
quered both any residual female-pattern body image issues and
all my new male-pattern body image issues that I'll be able to walk
through walls, but I won't, because I'll respect what the walls were
put in place to protect. I'll pay attention to only the meaningful,
character-building aspects of gender dysphoria (not that I support
the further medicalization of transition access by wanting to give
credence to the idea of gender dysphoria, I just use it as an easy
form of shorthand, but only around people who already intuitively
understand the broad collection of impulses/desires/needs I'm
referring to when I use the phrase) and never use transition as an
excuse to start indulging in self-loathing, or as justification for mis-
treating myself on the basis of garden-variety insecurities, or as a
basis to neglect my spiritual health or the well-being of the commu-
nities around me in order to chase after fleeting physical goals. And
my genitals? Why, terrific. Just terrific, thanks for asking.

"Thanks for saying something nice about my abs," I'll say, when
you invariably say something nice about my abs. In a very real way,
the fact that I've developed abs for the very first time after the age of
thirty-five will feel just like *you* have developed abs, and also simultaneously like you have freed yourself from the desire to chase abs
instead of learn to tend to and nurture your body as a secret garden.
"That really means a lot to me and my abs."

And you'll know we both really mean it.

CHAPTER 20

Paul and Second Timothy:
The Transmasculine Epistles

From Paul, who was bowled over in the street by God and never complained, to Timothy, my dearly beloved son: Grace, mercy, and peace. You headline my prayers, night and day, and I call to mind our transmasculine ancestors before addressing God directly, in gratitude and praise; greatly desiring to see you that I might be joyful again.

When I call to remembrance the root and the rock of faith within you, which you got from your grandmother Lois and your mother, Eunice, inasmuch as in your transition you have not attempted to divest yourself of what you have inherited from women. What good dwells in them, I am persuaded, dwells in thee also. *Within* thee, I should clarify! Looks-wise, you're so masc it makes my teeth hurt, but you've simultaneously managed to completely avoid any sort of performative, self-conscious masculinity, as God has not given us a spirit of anxiety but of power, and love, and of sound mind, that you need not be ashamed of me or of being weirdly religious sometimes. And as we have been called with a holy calling, not according to our own designs but according to his own purposes, which was given to us in Christ who transitioned before the world began (it *is* a cliché to say Christ transitioned as we have transitioned, and yet our own transitions were prefigured in his), wherefore I have been appointed a preacher, and an apostle, and a teacher.

Wherefore, if I'm honest, I have also been appointed suffering. But I'm not embarrassed by it—at least not beyond the standard, as the natural transmasculine condition is one of embarrassment— and neither should you be. Hold fast to the form of the sound words of faith and love we last exchanged with one another, that good thing that was committed to you by the Holy Ghost, and all of our friends with long names who are not afraid to greet us in public. Onesiphorus, for example. (I told him not to pick it, but . . . You know how it goes with they who are newly out; you can't tell them anything. There are those older in service and transition than me who counseled me not to write this epistle. *Give it a few years to settle, Paul,* they advised me; *just because you have a testosterone prescription and a new sense of exhilaration doesn't mean you have to go around setting down your life story, maybe save the memoir for next year.* Nuts to *them.*) Kindly do *not* give my regards to Phygelus and Hermogenes, and be sure to write back and let me know if they've registered the snub.

Anyhow, just a few reminders about your transition: be strong. If you hear people say nice things about me, as always, please feel free to pass that information along!! Be prepared to hear a great deal of unsolicited nonsense from all corners. Remember that we live together in the body of Christ first, then in the body of believers, then in the body individual; all are necessary. Deny none of them.

Remind the people that there's nothing wrong with having a set limit to how much time you want to dedicate as a community to wrangling over the specificities of language. Obviously you're all going to do some wrangling. I'm not saying *no* wrangling, I'm just saying maybe sometimes it will help to ask yourselves: Does this directly address material reality that isn't currently being served by preexisting language? And if the answer is "Not really," maybe you can all agree to move on. And if you *must* fight, assume that you both wish to do well, unless it's with an absolute human canker like Hymenaeus and Philetus, in which case do whatever you have to do, because I wouldn't believe them if they told me their own names.

Understand that the remedy to difficult times can be found in me: my teachings, my way of life, my purpose, my faith, my love, everything that happened to me, etc. And I could write a whole list of everyone who is *making* the times difficult, the boastful, the arrogant, the treacherous, the ones who chase recklessly after pleasure and call it *restoration*, everyone who wants to blame trans men generally and me specifically for the fact that they can't find a butch date in Antioch or Lystra, but you know who everybody is already, because nobody's half as good at concealing their worst impulse as they think they are. I know I sound difficult. Exacting. Petty, or pettish. Defensive. I'm sorry. It's been a long ministry, and I miss Lois, and I wish I hadn't fought so much with Phygelus, and I just don't want to see you make the same mistakes I made. Watch, and endure. Resist fables. Hold out for proof. God, I'm ready to sit down.

When it comes to my upcoming travel plans: You know how it is. Demas is finding himself in Thessalonica (??); Crescens is I have no idea where. It's basically me and Luke, which is what you get when you try communal living with only a verbal agreement to fall back on. So when you come visit please bring something we can all write on to turn back to when we all hate one another. And bring me something to wear I can actually fit in, I've been bulking. :)

Say hello to everybody, especially Onesiphorus. Everybody in Corinth says hi, even Claudia, who I didn't even think liked you. Now I must be about my father's business—

Paul. (I'm thinking of just going by P. What do you think? Once I started "passing"—not that I think the language of passing is, like, *tcch*, obviously it's just a certain type of shorthand and not something we should aspire to, *you* know what I mean—I started thinking that maybe I *am* more comfortable with flagging non-binary, so I'm trying out P for now, but just trying it out, thanks for witnessing this stage of my life journey.)

Paul.

Something Nice
Happens to Oedipus

Things were fine in Thebes. Laius was the king of Thebes and had a son with the princess Jocasta; the son was named Oedipus and he fulfilled things. (You know what they say about a man with swollen feet.) There were some allegations against Laius, but I wasn't there, and anyway, I'm sure it wasn't really that bad. People made the curse out to be a bigger deal than it was. But there *was* a curse on Laius. The curse was Daddy Issues. Only a daddy can have Daddy Issues.

The Daddy Issues of Laius include:

- insisting on taking your children hiking even after they start crying
- ignoring the collective good and stiffing oracles, who depend on tips
- refusing to save the city
- letting four attendants take the hit
- failing to bring a vehicle to a complete stop before proceeding into the intersection

Anyhow, the baby was a boy, so the king called a local shepherd to him and bade him carry the child to a lonely hill called Mount Cithaeron and leave him there. "Nail his feet to the mountain if you have to." A decision admittedly based on fear. But you can't base your happiness on someone else's behavior, and the baby Oedipus was found and carried to the palace of King Polybus of Corinth, whose Queen Merope had no child of her own and resolved to adopt the foundling, so everything ended up working out. A happy childhood is only ever a mountain and a set of nails away.

The boy grew up believing himself the true-born son of Corinth, until one day a drunk, banquet-roistered, said, "No, not quite." The young prince went to Delphi, tipped the oracle, and got a vague answer: "Shake hands with your father, have lunch with your mother. Don't overextend yourself."

Thinking this decree referred to Polybus and Merope, Oedipus left Corinth. There was no rush; he'd lunched with them both before. Quite nice lunches, too. They had sex with each other, Polybus and Merope. The complex, whatever complex there may be, has to include Polybus and Merope if it's going to include anyone. That's a mother and a father, too, right there.

It happened that this journey of Oedipus's took him to a place where two roads met. There he encountered an old man in a chariot, flanked by servants and preceded by a herald—a Bubble of Daddies. Oedipus was accustomed to being treated with deference. Good for him! The old man was also accustomed to being deferred to. (What have *you* grown accustomed to?) Oedipus refused to pull his chariot aside when ordered to do so by the herald, who thereupon killed one of his horses.

"Oh," said Oedipus. "Oh, oh, oh." A dead horse can really change your perspective on forward momentum. So he stepped out of his chariot and shook hands with the old man, the herald, and the rest of the attendants. "Please don't worry about it," he said when they tried to apologize about the horse. "If I change the way I look at things, the things I look at change. Please, go ahead. I'm a stranger and a guest here." The old man was Laius, king of Thebes, and he invited the young man—one so capable of rapid-onset restraint— to return with him to the city.

The city had a monster; the monster was a Sphinx; the Sphinx asked everyone questions they didn't know the answer to. The monster wore a woman's face and a woman's shoulders but stopped being a woman after that and started being something else. She had very bad posture and lived on a rock and no one knew how to talk to her. As Oedipus rightly pointed out, there are worse things than not knowing the answer to something, so everyone decided to leave her alone. Some people nail themselves to mountains and don't come down for anything.

The king invited the young man who'd been so understanding at the crossroads out to lunch. None of them thought much of it afterward, and nobody had sex.

Maybe the king and queen did; I don't know. They were married to each other, and it's none of our business.

(It's weird that you would even ask about this. Other people don't think about these things. Why are you like this?)

Later it came out they were all related. As the details couldn't possibly affect you and your life, there's no need to trot them all out.

So everything ended up working out pretty well, all things considered. It just goes to show that sometimes perfectly nice things can happen at a crossroads, especially if you're polite and willing to listen, and don't get too bent out of shape if something happens to your horse. Everyone still died, but much later, and not too unpleasantly, except for the horse.

CHAPTER 21

Destry Rides Again, or Jimmy Stewart Has a Body and So Do I

There's something truly wonderful about referring to a procedure as specific as a bilateral mastectomy with a term as blandly ominous as "top surgery."

Is it serious, Doc?

Yeah, son. I'm afraid there's nothing to do but schedule you for top surgery.

What parts of me will be affected, Doc?

The top.

What are you gonna do to the top of me?

Surgery. We're going in and we're gonna have to surger your Top.

"Just get rid of the whole thing, Doctor," I imagined myself saying generously, swinging my legs from the examination table. "Take the whole top off. I want my neighbors to have a clear view to the sea. Give it away to those deserving unfortunates who may have no top to speak of. I'll get by just fine with a bottom and a middle. No top for me—I'll get by."

One thinks of it less as a removal than as an installation, or having one thing hauled away to make room for something else, the more time passes. In the months and years since I had/underwent/

experienced/paid for/submitted to/achieved top surgery at a clinic in Plano, Texas, I've been able to experience something physically that I had previously only had scope to imagine. There is, as I had suspected but did not know until I had done it, a great deal of difference between imagining one's chest *without* something and encountering a wholly new physical plane. I had been very anxious in the months leading up to the surgery itself, often stopping to ask myself if I wanted to postpone or even cancel the appointment altogether. Without making claims on what I may or may not feel about my body in the future, I can say that doubt and uncertainty seemed to leave me the day I exchanged imagination for experience. Now that I have a new kind of embodied knowledge about my own chest I might sometimes experience wistfulness, or a sense of poignancy, or curiosity about various alternatives, but it is not a chest I feel uncertain about any longer.

"Yes, of course not, you cut the uncertainty *off*," might be the reply if this were part of a vaudeville routine, which it isn't.

But at any rate, I've developed a different sort of relationship to uncertainty, one where I no longer consider avoiding change to be the highest good. I may have various changing thoughts and opinions and reactions to myself—my body, my future, my past, the things I want, the things I fear, the things I want to want—but having tested one uncertain theory, I flinch less at the prospect of others. It's a new chest for me, rather than simply an altered or a pared-down version of my old one, and I've had a new chest before, so even in the newness there is a kind of familiarity. The first new chest was given to me by my endocrine system (I assume; I'm no expert, and it may be that the endocrine system is simply an old superstition designed to scare children) around the age of twelve, and I accepted it then with relatively good humor and a sense of resignation. I accepted the second at thirty-one with great joy and a number of bookmarked tabs about changing surgical dressings.

In the first few weeks of recovery after top surgery, I spent a lot of time watching old movies. It did not make sense, at least in my mind, to think of myself as *recovering* from anything, because from almost the first moment I came to it seemed as if there had never been anything about my chest that would have required surgical intervention in the first place. This reality was more believable than what had come before. This is a line of thinking that my mind is more easily convinced of than my body. About nine or ten days afterward I started feeling pretty well most of the time, and could once again gingerly hold my own coffee cup and open silverware drawers on my own behalf. But there's a good long distance between feeling no longer freshly incised and being able to resume normal activities, and I was under doctor's orders to restrict myself to "*T. rex*–style arm movements," which meant I spent a lot of afternoons watching old movies on the couch in a spirit of mild-to-moderate agitation. Miles and miles of adorable new chest, and a tired body that wouldn't deliver it anywhere without protest.

I had a friend visiting from out of town who was doing things like cleaning out the litterbox (for the cat) and opening jars (for me) and in the course of conversation it came up that they'd never seen *Destry Rides Again*, despite being a big fan of Madeline Kahn's performance in *Blazing Saddles*, modeled after Marlene Dietrich in the same, so the two of us watched it together. Grace and I had been explaining our T4T energy theory to this friend, and I'd been trying to look for examples beyond the usual "short, anxious men" and "statuesque blond women" pairing.

When Jimmy Stewart as Tom Destry Jr steps down from the coach in Bottleneck for the first time, it's on the strength of his reputation as a lawman like his father. The man who's been riding in the coach next to him has been angry at the driver the whole trip, and the first thing he does is punch the guy in the jaw before shooting a gun out of the postilion's hand. Everyone applauds, assuming this is the new deputy, truly his father's son in name and deed, but of course it isn't—Jimmy steps onto the street carrying a canary in a birdcage and a woman's parasol. The case for Jimmy Stewart's transmasculinity as Tom Destry is, I think, a straightforward one: he's easily distinguished by his unusual height, immediately mistaken for someone else, bears a conflicted relationship to his father's legacy, constantly offers folksy, rambling, Christ-style parables about something that once happened to "a friend" in order to defuse tension (if you know a trans man, odds are good that you also know a trans man who's currently in seminary even though he isn't necessarily religious himself. Lord knows why, but it often seems to go with the territory. I'm not saying every guy who goes to seminary is trans, nor even that most trans guys sooner or later find themselves pursuing a doctrinal education, just that if you scratch enough trans men, eventually a seminarian will turn up).

There's a moment in the movie where Charles Winninger—Sheriff Washington Dimsdale—tearfully breaks down in front of Jimmy Stewart once his great plan to prove everybody wrong and clean up the town once and for all has fallen apart. It was a one-point plan, destined for failure: Call Tom Destry. That was all he had, and once that didn't work, he was left with nothing.

"Oh, Tom," he cries. "The only reason they made me sheriff here is because I was the town drunk. They wanted someone they could kick around, someone who wouldn't ask questions. But I was aimin' to fool 'em, do things right, send in for you. And now, you fooled me."

That day I watched *Destry Rides Again* with my friend I was exactly five years sober, and watching a man-who-is-not-a-man cradle a terrified drunk and say, "Well, you *will* fool them, Wash. We'll fool them together," was deeply moving to me, a man who has spent much of his life having exactly one plan upon which all my hopes rest, and falling to pieces when the plan (just four drinks tonight, just a haircut and hope nobody notices, disavow all desires and hope for the best) falls apart. I think there are better ways to talk about transition and sobriety than to only focus on one's feelings; *sola sentimente* is no better a foundation for transition than *sola scriptura* was for Protestantism. But it is true to say that I could not be a drunk and a man at the same time. The drunk was there to kick around and make sure no one asked questions; the drunk had to give way to make room—though that's not to say that I neatly and immediately swapped one out for the other, either. The point of my drunkenness was to forestall imagination; imagination was the first step on the road to action and action was dangerous. Better to ruminate, to nurse over old hurts, to rehearse again and again things that had already happened and could not be changed. Just as top surgery was about something more than merely removing part of my chest, sobriety required more than simply quitting drinking and carrying on otherwise as if nothing had changed. It required imagination, and imagination necessitates acknowledging that the future exists on its own terms and in its own right, and might even reach out and make demands of the present.

Anyhow, Tom Destry's great plan for Bottleneck is something along the lines of few-to-no guns, but plenty of incarceration, which is not much of an improvement in many ways. But in the world of the movie at least, he's unique in wanting to spend a great deal of time thinking before he does or says anything, unique in prioritizing imagination and possibility before moving ahead.

Grace and I talk often about what we thought about each other the day we met, when I asked her if she wanted to be best friends and she said that she did. The two of us looked very different then than we do now, but still recognized each other on sight. When Jimmy Stewart meets Marlene Dietrich—a German woman inexplicably nicknamed "Frenchy" in a Western boomtown, tricking drunk ranch hands into gambling away their life savings, stealing men's pants and sucker-punching their wives—they both spend a lot of time sizing each other up, trying to figure out who's got the upper hand, and if the upper hand is worth getting.

"How's the weather up there?" she says to him on sight, looking up at his great height. *"How's the weather up there,"* he says at the exact same time in a weary tone. "Ah, come on. You can do better than that." Marlene never exactly tells him that he can do better, too, but she does hurl a number of glass bottles at his head, which communicates the same general principle. There are moments in the movie where Grace is very much Marlene, and moments where I am very much Jimmy, but there are two moments, I think, where we switch.

The first switch comes when Tom Destry visits Frenchy in her dressing room and says, "Now, I bet you got kind of a lovely face under all that paint there. Why don't you wipe it off someday and have a good look? Figure out how you can live up to it." Most of the sentiment behind the idea of makeup as a face-obliterating mask we can cheerfully leave in 1939, of course, but the work of figuring out how to live up to one's face is no joke. The first time I ever used a men's bathroom in public was at a grocery store. I'd been transitioning at this point for a little while but dithering on the subject of which door to duck behind. Grace—still, at this point, my best friend and not my girlfriend—pushed me through the door. She was on the other side, a little pale, when I came out a minute later, all certainty gone: "Oh God, did I read that moment right?" (She had; everything was just fine; I don't recommend that you shove any of your loved ones into any bathrooms, but it worked for us in that moment. All public bathrooms are terrible, but men's rooms are terrible in an entirely new way.)

Destry is a man who is not like other men in Bottleneck, and Frenchy is not like the other women there, either. There is more to transition than that not-being-like, but there's some *there* there;

they have a dissimilar and yet a shared sense of uniqueness. She notices his height, and he notices her face. He is stymied in certain ways; she is self-sabotaging in others. They both like each other very much.

The second time the two of us switch our sense of identification is the moment Frenchy dies. (Another sentiment we can happily leave in 1939.) She sags into Jimmy's arms and wipes the lipstick off her mouth before asking him to kiss her. He tilts his hat before he does, so that no one else, not even the audience at home, can watch them do it. And without suggesting that removing makeup is the same thing as removing artifice or becoming honest, I knew myself to be Frenchy, not Destry, in that moment: ready to ask for privacy and intimacy at the same time. The year I asked for top surgery, five years into sobriety, was the first time I admitted publicly to having a body and wanting to do something about it, something I could not, or at least had not, done before. Part of the reason I did not think of top surgery as being primarily organized around any sort of removal, at least physically, was because I thought of there being more of me afterward, rather than less.

A STRONG CASE FOR T4T ENERGY IN A CONVERSATION BETWEEN GRACE AND MYSELF

SELF: [*Unspecified acknowledgment of surprising, yet obvious, new hormonally charged reality that is both true physically and beyond the physical*].

GRACE: If someone else had made a claim about [*unspecified acknowledgment of surprising, yet obvious, new hormonally charged reality that is both true physically and beyond the physical*] before I started hormones, I would not have believed them. But if you had said it to me, I would have believed you.

SELF: [*Wipes makeup off and dies triumphantly in her arms.*]

GRACE: You are being dramatic. Wake up and finish this
conversation.

SELF: [*Cracking a single eye open*] I am willing to sing two
bars of "Something There," but I don't think I can get
any less oblique than that.

GRACE: Ah, come on. You can do better than that.

SELF: I am willing and able to acknowledge that you have a
body, and that I have a body, and that yours is good,
and mine. This is more than I have ever done. The
weather up here is fine.

GRACE: Now, I bet you got kind of a lovely face under all
that paint there. Why don't you wipe it off someday
and have a good look? Figure out how you can live
up to it.

Fin.

Toward the end of *Destry Rides Again,* just before the credits roll,
when Destry is being set up in an obvious marriage-plot moment
with a different kind of girl, he defers with another story. I love this
moment because it suggests that he considers heterosexual marriage to be a threat just as serious, and just as need of a solution, as
gun violence: "Y'know, speaking of marriage . . . I had a friend once
that happened to . . ." She looks disappointed. He keeps talking, trying to defuse the situation. It's Marlene or nobody, and it looks like
Jimmy is ready to stick with nobody—and by extension the whole
town of Bottleneck.

Later, director (not *their* director, merely *a* director) Peter Bogdanovich would claim that Marlene and Jimmy had an on-set affair
that resulted in Marlene's getting pregnant. His source was, supposedly, Orson Welles, who also claimed to have taken her to get an
abortion without Stewart's knowledge. In some ways I have diffi-

culty believing that out of all her friends, Marlene would choose Orson Welles to confide in about her romantic relationships; in other ways I have no difficulty believing it at all. I once saw Bogdanovich give one of his "Life with Orson Welles" talks in Hollywood, and he said one of his fondest memories was looking up from his desk in his home office to see Orson tearing through the halls, shouting, "*Dick Van Dyke* is on!" And I had no trouble believing *that*, so perhaps it's not too difficult to believe the rest.

The Matriarchs of Avonlea Begrudgingly Accept Your Transition / Men of *Anne of Green Gables* Experience

DRAMATIS PERSONAE
RACHEL LYNDE, *as efficient and sure-minded as God*
MARILLA CUTHBERT, *formidable, earthy, winsome*
THE AUTHOR, *uncertain*

> **RACHEL LYNDE:** Mind that I was against taking the boy in from the start; orphans, especially redheaded ones, are always exactly the kind who do end up transitioning, and the only thing I can think of that's worse than a redheaded *girl* child is a redheaded *boy* one.
>
> **THE AUTHOR, POINTEDLY:** If it helps, I think I'm going bald early.
>
> **RACHEL LYNDE:** It doesn't, of course. Well, instead of being hopeless in the kitchen, maybe he can go be hopeless in the fields for a bit, until we can figure out

just exactly what part of Green Gables he's capable of being something other than hopeless in.

MARILLA CUTHBERT: I don't mind saying that I think he's turned into a real fine boy. And I don't mind saying that I'm proud of him, either.

RACHEL LYNDE: Does raise some tricky questions about the Blythe boy and the Barry girl, don't it, though?

MARILLA CUTHBERT: Does it?

THE AUTHOR, POINTEDLY: Yes, does it?

RACHEL LYNDE: I can see I've stepped into a real nest of it today. Didn't know male wasps carried stingers, too.

MARILLA CUTHBERT: [*As if nothing had happened*] I can't say I saw it coming, but then many a good turn has come from a surprise.

RACHEL LYNDE: Lord knows I enjoy a surprise myself. But if anyone was going to end up that way, I would have put good money on it being—

MARILLA CUTHBERT: [*Loudly*] He'd been worried, some, about how Matthew would take it, for fear that there'd be a distance put between them.

RACHEL LYNDE: As if Matthew wouldn't find a way to spoil him regardless.

MARILLA CUTHBERT: I thought it was nonsense, too.

RACHEL LYNDE: And I hear a number of Redmond students are doing it now. So he'll have—I expect—company in the spring. Not to say it's faddish, exactly, but then who wants to be an iconoclast?

MARILLA CUTHBERT: Fad or no fad, once he puts his mind to something, it usually carries the day.

RACHEL LYNDE: Lord, yes. Whatever else might change, that red hair is mighty determined. Can see it coming from a mile away.

CHAPTER 22

The Opposite of Baptism

Thus having pass'd the night in fruitless pain,
I to my longing friends return again,
Amaz'd th' augmented number to behold,
Of men and matrons mix'd, of young and old;
A wretched exil'd crew together brought,
With arms appointed, and with treasure fraught,
Resolv'd, and willing, under my command,
To run all hazards both of sea and land.
The Morn began, from Ida, to display
Her rosy cheeks; and Phosphor led the day:
Before the gates the Grecians took their post,
And all pretense of late relief was lost.
I yield to Fate, unwillingly retire,
And, loaded, up the hill convey my sire.

—*The Aeneid, Book II*, translated by John Dryden

There are two accounts of how persons came to be in the book of Genesis, as it retells the making of them: first as a pair (Gen 1:26–28), later in sequence (Gen 2:7–24). The first is, perhaps unsurprisingly, my favorite. The story of creation is full of the pleasures of accuracy-in-naming—not quite "I calls 'em like I see 'em," neither so idiosyncratic nor so defensive an attitude, but in taking correct measure *of* and full responsibility *for* things. The pleasures of the person Eve-and-Adam, who was both a community and a worker, came in cataloging, in identifying, in recognizing, in naming, in affirming—God's work among God's creatures. Labels that *suggest vocation*, rather than labels that *restrict ability*, if one is skeptical of labels.

> *Then God said, "Let Us make man in Our image, according to Our likeness; let them have dominion over the fish of the sea, over the birds of the air, and over the cattle, over all the earth and over every creeping thing that creeps on the earth." So God created man in His own image; in the image of God He created him; male and female He created them. Then God blessed them, and God said to them, "Be fruitful and multiply; fill the earth and subdue it; have dominion over the fish of the sea, over the birds of the air, and over every living thing that moves on the earth."*
>
> —Gen. 1:26–28

Let us call this act *empersoning* rather than *impersonation*. God begins the task of *empersoning* by speaking to himself, by making a delightful announcement and establishing the number of gifts he plans on giving someone else, then lists all the things he has already made in a pleasurable recitation. Persons are unlike creatures, in this account of creation, and yet they are recognizable and known to one another, and bear different kinds of responsibility to one another. Persons have been given the task of creating more joys and pleasures in an already pleasurable world, of exploring, of establishing meaningful authority, of establishing care, of identifying life and offering it the rights and privileges that are all life's due; one might spend a great deal of time examining the word "subdue" but I don't especially care to. One might summarize this portion of Genesis as: *there are many good ways to relate to everything that experiences life differently than oneself; persons have been tasked by a creative principle to explore them all.*

I don't remember who first claimed that the voice one uses to talk to animals is the voice one would like to use to speak to oneself; it sounds vaguely plausible in the way that most of my horoscopes do, but also a bit too neat to provide the whole story. But every dog I have ever lived with has made it clear to me that my desire for cheerful narration as I perform the tasks necessary to self-replication (cleaning, eating, stretching, drinking, walking, doing the washing-up, ignoring my mail, hormone injection, making tea) is immense, and it requires a dog in order to work; if I say those things to myself I feel ridiculous and infantilized, and if I say it to another human being, I'd likely (and rightly) be begged to knock it off. But a dog's capacity to absorb repetition is equally immense, and in this way persons and dogs are uniquely suited to one another. There is no end to a dog's ability to receive acts of affection and reassurance throughout the day. A dog delights in establishing comfort and meeting its physical needs in ways I often forget, avoid, attempt to draw out, or manipulate in myself.

In the second account of the creation of persons, God "causes a deep sleep to fall on Adam so he slept; and He took one of his ribs, and closed up the flesh in its place," which is both too on the nose an analogy for top surgery to be worth bothering with, and too obvious a reference to Marilyn Manson supposedly getting some of his ribs removed so as to more efficiently suck his own dick; an effectively contentless Bible reference. This version, too, so often seems to cause people to lose their heads and attempt to draw conclusions about why, say, men are hardwired not to notice the little blinking light that means the dishwasher is ready to unload, the better to serve the Lord, or why women make especially good part-time social workers, because the rib is the most compassionate and curved of all the parts of the human skeleton, or similar nonsense. But it too is a story of a shared body, of like and unlike, of bones and flesh held in common, of naming and separation and distinction and community; there is good in this telling of the story, too.

Grace, who has previously appeared throughout this book first as an unnamed friend, then as my girlfriend, is now my wife; we were married shortly before I finished the manuscript. At the time, I understood our wedding as symbolizing the crowning (or at least penultimate) addition to an already large family; she is now the only family member with whom I have a relationship, a development that has been both completely devastating and entirely necessary. We both took public steps toward transition within a few months of each other, and hers has been consistent in a way mine has not. Every so often we seek reassurance from each other that it is not necessary for our transitions to serve as equal and opposite reactions to each other, that we are not violating a strict one-in-one-out policy, that what we hold in common is a commitment to autonomy, moral sanity, and pleasure. The fear that one day I will affirm a commitment to pleasure and autonomy that finally and inexorably alienates me from the approval of my family is now gone. I find the absence of this fear exhilarating and deeply disorienting, as it has acted as a counterweight on me for my entire adult life.

I fear—how could I not?—that I will merely replace one error with another, that I will take avowal of desire in itself as an unalloyed, uncomplicated good in all places and in all situations, that no matter what I try to make of my life, I will never be free of that counterweight, whether I ever speak to another member of my family of origin again—always reacting, equally and oppositely, to someone else's commitments. I have changed my name, first, middle, and last, several times over. At present I have taken my wife's last name as my own and have said, a little desperately, "No matter what happens between us, I'm staying a Lavery," more than once. There are many good ways to relate to the world, except the way I was raised in—where then to begin seeking out new forms of relation, and against what should I try to rate these methods, having no organizing basis of comparison?

As a child, I belonged to a denomination that discouraged infant baptism but encouraged "adult" baptism beginning at the age of twelve; it perhaps goes without saying that I was not encouraged to make any other "adult" decisions on my own behalf at that age by either my family or the church to which we belonged. Plenty of twelve-year-olds spend a little time in a lake, of course; in a very real sense there's nothing particularly unusual about my having been briefly dunked underwater the summer after sixth grade, and subsequently I have little to complain about. But I cannot shake the sense that I have only recently sprung from being held underwater, unsure whether I have been released or struggled my own way out or simply found myself, like all human beings, naturally and instinctively buoyant. If one finds ground to stand upon, it so follows that the rest of the river is but shallow; thus we get over.

Acknowledgments

I'm deeply grateful to my agent, Kate McKean, for helping me write a book unlike anything I've written before, as well as editor Rakesh Satyal for bearing with me during a number of identity crises that this collection was merely "memoir-adjacent" and not a full-bore autobiography. I'm also grateful to my longtime business soulmate, Nicole Cliffe, for thinking carefully and speaking lovingly about our changing relationship to sisterhood, which has been a source of great joy and affirmation to me.

I'd like to thank Flan Joel, Peyton Thomas, Isaac Fellman, Calvin Kasulke, Colette Arrand, and Frances Hocutt for helping to sharpen and refine my ideas about trans narratives. Additional thanks are due to the following men, mostly fictional, for inspiring my transition: William Shatner's roles on both *Star Trek* and *Columbo*, André 3000's wardrobe, Rufus Wainwright (particularly the *Rufus Does Judy At Carnegie Hall* album), Johnny Weir at the 2010 Winter Olympics, Brendan Fraser in the late 1990s, and the entire cast of *The Outsiders*. Thank you all for being so attractive that it changed the trajectory of my life.

I thank the good Lord, who made me trans, and *who is faithful and will not let you be tried beyond your strength; but with the trial will also make a way to escape, that you may be able to bear it,* 1 Cor. 10:13.

To Grace Elisabeth Lavery, whose own transition has served as a model for rigorous thinking, personal vitality, the ruthless pursuit of joy and acceptance, I am truly and immeasurably grateful. There is no reader whose judgment I prize more. I am at my best when I push myself to keep up with you; it is a delight, an honor, and a meaningful challenge to be married to you. Thank you for being so attractive that it changed the trajectory of my life.

About the Author

Daniel Alexander Mallory Ortberg is a cofounder of *The Toast* and the author of *Texts From Jane Eyre* and *The Merry Spinster*. He currently serves as the advice columnist Dear Prudence for *Slate* and lives in California.